ASSESSMENT FOR DYSLEXIA AND LEARNING DIFFERENCES

by the same author

The Big Book of Dyslexia Activities for Kids and Teens
100+ Creative, Fun, Multi-sensory and Inclusive Ideas for Successful Learning
Gavin Reid, Nick Guise and Jennie Guise
ISBN 978 1 78592 377 7
eISBN 978 1 78450 725 1

Dyslexia in the Early Years
A Handbook for Practice
Gavin Reid
ISBN 978 1 78592 065 3
eISBN 978 1 78450 327 7

of related interest

Fun Games and Activities for Children with Dyslexia
How to Learn Smarter with a Dyslexic Brain
Alais Winton
Illustrated by Joe Salerno
ISBN 978 1 78592 292 3
eISBN 978 1 78450 596 7

The Illustrated Guide to Dyslexia and Its Amazing People
Kate Power and Kathy Iwanczak Forsyth
Foreword by Richard Rogers
ISBN 978 1 78592 330 2
eISBN 978 1 78450 647 6

Dyslexia is My Superpower (Most of the Time)
Margaret Rooke
Forewords by Professor Catherine Drennan and Loyle Carner
ISBN 978 1 78592 299 2
eISBN 978 1 78450 606 3

Dyslexia and Spelling
Making Sense of It All
Kelli Sandman-Hurley
ISBN 978 1 78592 791 1
eISBN 978 1 78450 760 2

ASSESSMENT FOR DYSLEXIA AND LEARNING DIFFERENCES

A CONCISE GUIDE FOR TEACHERS AND PARENTS

Gavin Reid and Jennie Guise

Jessica Kingsley *Publishers*
London and Philadelphia

First published in 2019
by Jessica Kingsley Publishers
73 Collier Street
London N1 9BE, UK
and
400 Market Street, Suite 400
Philadelphia, PA 19106, USA

www.jkp.com

Library of Congress Cataloging in Publication Data
A CIP catalog record for this book is available from the Library of Congress

British Library Cataloguing in Publication Data
A CIP catalogue record for this book is available from the British Library

ISBN 978 1 78592 522 1
eISBN 978 1 78450 911 8

Printed and bound in Great Britain

Contents

Introduction

We are delighted to have the opportunity to write this book on dyslexia assessment for parents. We have both had experiences as parents, and fully appreciate the challenges and the paths that children and young people have to follow from early childhood to secondary school, further education and the workplace.

We appreciate that being dyslexic can add a different dimension to those challenges. We have also had substantial experience working with parents of children with dyslexia, and through this we have become very aware of the challenges that parents can experience in relation to the educational needs of children with dyslexia, and the type of advice they most readily benefit from.

With substantial experience in teaching at a range of levels, we are also aware of the needs of the education sector, and of the importance of effective communication between home and school. These experiences, and our current work practices as psychologists and consultants, have influenced our desire to write this book for parents.

We strongly believe that 'home' and 'school' should be constructively linked, so this book is also aimed at classroom teachers who may not have specialist training in the area of assessment for dyslexia and other learning differences. It is important that home and school are linked, and this type of book can contribute to that.

We have included the term 'learning differences' in the title of this book for very good reasons. We have always contended that dyslexia is not a disability, and in some cases it can facilitate abilities and skills that may elude other children. The term 'learning difference' is a very accurate one because dyslexia is exactly that – a difference in how children learn, how they process information and work out problems, and a difference in skills areas. For example, they may find reading particularly challenging, but they may be able to carry out some visual or computer tasks with minimal support and intervention.

For that reason, it is important to view the child as a whole, and not to judge him or her simply on reading performance! Additionally, in all children, different parts of the brain develop at different rates. Research has shown that the parts of the brain that are involved in the reading process may be constructed differently, and be more difficult to access, in children with dyslexia. In other words, to adopt a very commonly used phrase, they may be 'wired differently'. This can make some tasks straightforward, and others challenging. We, as parents and educators, need to acknowledge these differences, and appreciate that a challenge with reading does not mean that the child is unable to learn!

Having a 'learning difference' is therefore a more accurate descriptive term to describe a child with dyslexia. It is important that parents, teachers and the person him- or herself realise that. This term also highlights the positive aspects of dyslexia, and that individuals with dyslexia can have talents in some areas, even though literacy might be at a lower level. A 'learning difference' is therefore a more accurate term than a 'learning difficulty'.

It is also very important to note that a child might have a learning difference (for example, due to a slower speed of processing, or difficulties with working memory) and not be dyslexic. These children will often benefit from many of the types of support and accommodation that are described in this book.

In this book, we will be covering some of the key factors that can represent learning differences, and specifically the criteria for a dyslexic profile. At the same time, we highlight the need to take a broader view of dyslexia and not to focus on only a few specific factors. Although there has been a great deal of publicity about dyslexia, with organisations such as the British Dyslexia Association (BDA) spearheading campaigns including the annual Dyslexia Awareness Week, there is still a surprising amount of ignorance and misunderstanding around. We hope this book will help to clear up any misunderstandings, and give parents the information, understanding and guidance to help them steer a course toward successful and positive educational outcomes for their children.

The book will provide information on the importance of assessment, obtaining an assessment, and the type of follow-up that can result from an assessment. There is now an increasing range of resources, websites and commercially driven resources and programmes for dyslexia, and it is important that parents have a clear understanding of their child's needs through a full assessment before embarking on any intervention. That is also why it is important to link with schools, and to work on developing the child's literacy and learning skills together.

In some cases, there is still, however, a gap between the child's and the parents' needs and school provision. Some of this may be real, and some more to do with a difference in perspective, but whatever the reason, it is crucial that children's and parents' needs are not ignored. There is a growing desire for independent assessments – quite separate from the school – and these, as well as in-school assessments, have a key role to play. Both will be considered and discussed in this book.

Parents, and indeed teachers, may well experience some confusion with the language that assessors use in reports and in feedback from an assessment. We hope to explain and clarify some of the terms used in an assessment, in order to equip parents with the understanding and the confidence to recognise their child's needs following an assessment, and to be in a position to ensure that these needs are met.

We both have experience in working in many different continents and countries. We appreciate that dyslexia assessment is an international concern, and one that parents – wherever they live – will have a desire to find out more about. Although assessment reports may vary from country to country, the principles, and many of the terms, are similar, so we are directing the focus of this book to an international audience. We hope that this will help to develop confidence and reassurance in parents, and give them the direction and guidance to steer a positive educational path for their children, wherever they live.

About This Book

Chapter 1: What Is Dyslexia?

Although we appreciate that many readers will have some understanding of dyslexia, we have not assumed this, and this chapter will provide essentially an introduction to dyslexia. We have included a brief overview of some key aspects in current research in dyslexia, as well as definitions. We find that parents often ask about the key research areas and current definitions of dyslexia. We also discuss the range of challenges that can be experienced by young people with dyslexia and provide a range of characteristics that can be associated with dyslexia. We also provide information on how to obtain an assessment.

Many of the points in this chapter will be followed up in later chapters, but we intended here to provide an initial outline of dyslexia and, importantly, what an assessment can provide. In the next chapter, we look at dyslexia from the child's point of view.

Chapter 2: Being Dyslexic

This chapter captures some of the experiences of children with dyslexia. It also highlights the importance of constructive and ongoing communication between home and school, and the child him- or herself should be involved here. Although we stress the positive aspects of dyslexia, we appreciate that being dyslexic is not always a 'bed of roses'! We have ensured that the potential negative aspects of dyslexia are considered, because it is only by knowing how dyslexia affects the individual that we, as responsible adults, can provide the right level of support at the right time.

In addition to discussing support, this chapter also refers to self-knowledge; it is important for children with dyslexia to be aware of their learning differences, and to develop learning strategies that are best suited to them! We have provided a number of first-hand accounts from people with dyslexia, and the frustrations experienced can be seen here. It is also important to realise that these tough times may have helped them to become more successful, and more independent learners. There is no doubt that the child in school struggling with dyslexia will require support of varying degrees while at the same time they strive for self-knowledge and independence in learning. This is the aim, but it will not happen overnight, and it certainly will not happen without support and understanding from the adults who are in a position to help.

This is followed up in the next chapter, on the purpose of an assessment, which also looks at the key factors that can emerge from an assessment and essentially provides the reader with insights into what can be expected from an assessment.

Chapter 3: The Purpose of an Assessment

Obtaining an assessment, whether it is through school or done independently, can be quite a concerning time for parents. Many do not know what to expect, and the impact it might have on their child. It is important at the outset to indicate what the purpose of the assessment is, and how the results will be used. For that reason, we have placed this chapter early in the book. We indicate what an assessment should provide, and very importantly the type of feedback that parents should expect. What we are also highlighting in this chapter is the importance of obtaining a learning profile, because this can provide pointers to intervention and indeed any diagnosis. Obtaining a profile is one of the key reasons for an assessment. It can pinpoint the type and extent of intervention that the child will require.

We have also indicated in this chapter that an assessment may well provide a diagnosis and this – if appropriate – is also important, and will have implications for intervention. If the profile points to an assessment of dyslexia, then this should be stated; parents and teachers need to know this.

This chapter leads us to Chapter 4, which describes the process of the assessment.

Chapter 4: The Assessment Process

We are fully aware that the process of the assessment can differ from country to country, and also from school to school. Additionally, the type of assessment that is to be carried out can also influence the process. For example, the assessment may be based on tests carried out in school, or independently outwith the school. It might use observation and/or checklists. Clearly, the process can be different in the different circumstances of the assessment. Nevertheless, there are some core elements to the assessment process, whether it is carried out in school or independently, and we have described them here. In this chapter, we describe the different types of assessment and the process the assessment will follow, and we indicate the type of learning profile that can emerge from the assessment. We also discuss the role that parents can play in the assessment. Irrespective of what type of assessment is carried out, it is imperative that pointers for intervention are made clear at the conclusion of the assessment.

Chapter 5: Assessment and Impact on Learning

In this chapter, we follow up on the previous chapter, and discuss in some detail the different forms of assessment. We focus on the kinds of difficulties that children with dyslexia experience across the curriculum, as well as in the reading process. This leads to recommendations that can be carried out at school, and also consideration of how different aspects of the curriculum can be adapted to suit children with dyslexia. This type of information is relevant to parents as well as teachers. Parents will inevitably need to attend school meetings to discuss their child's progress. It is therefore important for them, and for teachers, to be aware of the barriers that can prevent their child from accessing the full curriculum.

One of the themes of this chapter is communication between home and school. If this is to be effective, teachers need to be aware of the barriers to learning that dyslexic children experience, and parents must be informed of how the school can support the child throughout the curriculum to overcome these barriers.

In this chapter, we have also referred to other and often overlapping conditions, such as dyspraxia, dysgraphia and (central) auditory processing difficulties. We conclude with some specific suggestions for parents, and specifically some suggestions for technology and apps that can be used to support the child with dyslexia. This area of strategies and technology is followed up in the next chapter on strategies and resources.

Chapter 6: Strategies and Resources

This chapter will provide a reference for parents and for teachers on tips and strategies to help the dyslexic learner. Here, we discuss reading, spelling, handwriting, written expression and numeracy and we provide some explanation and the rationale that underpins some of these strategies.

We also look at cognitive aspects, such as working memory and processing speed, and we discuss the accommodations and supports that can be used if the child has difficulties in these areas. We also consider self-esteem and overall confidence, and the importance of these factors for successful outcomes. In other words, we can have all the resources in the world at hand, but if the child is not ready, or able, to access these due to low self-esteem, then the effort can be wasted. The first priority is therefore to look for ways of building up self-esteem and confidence, and introduce activities that can bring success. The experience of success can pave the way for further success, and ultimately a positive approach to independent learning.

Chapter 7: Assessment – Summary

We are aware that there is a great deal of information in this book – much of which may well be new to parents and some teachers. We have therefore highlighted the key points in this final chapter, and in doing so we have felt the need to introduce some new information. So, the chapter is more than a summing up – it is a summary of the area of assessment and intervention for children with learning differences. We refer to school policies, as well as factors relating to independent assessments. We also make references here to the role of parents and the importance of feedback.

Appendices

In Appendix 1, we describe the main tests that can be used in an assessment, and some key factors about these.

To help parents more fully understand the sometimes rather confusing terminology used in discussions and in some reports, we have included a glossary of common terms in Appendix 2.

We have provided some useful contacts in Appendix 3. This list is not exhaustive, and it is a good idea for you to make your own list and specifically to add some local contacts.

Many parents now seek out an independent assessment. This can have a number of uses, particularly if the family is moving to another area or country, or if the child is moving to another sector, for example transitioning between different types of school. Parents, however, can be quite confused by the terminology and detail in some reports. Some of the more technical phrasing is often necessary when the report is also being used to justify extra academic support, or accommodations in exams and tests. While we appreciate that reports may be styled differently, and the content will vary, we have provided in Appendix 4 some guidance for parents on how to interpret the assessment report. We have detailed the main content areas, and provided explanations of some of the technical words that can be used in reports. We hope this appendix will help to clear up any confusion (and anxieties) that parents may experience when reading such reports.

Chapter 1

What Is Dyslexia?

Dyslexia can affect reading, writing, spelling, arithmetic/mathematical skills, memory, processing information, processing speed and organisation. There may also be evidence of poor written expression, which can often contrast with the child's competence in oral expression, although this is not always the case. Dyslexia can also be referred to as a 'learning difference', and not necessarily a 'learning difficulty'. At the same time, one cannot, and should not, underestimate the challenges faced by the child with dyslexia, and the challenges and concerns shared by parents, and of course teachers, who have to understand and support children with dyslexia in the classroom.

Defining dyslexia

There are a number of definitions of dyslexia, and a number of different characteristics. Dyslexia is not a single entity (nor does it stem from a single gene). Dyslexia is multi-faceted, and that can explain why a single, universally accepted definition has not yet been achieved. The following factors can be associated with dyslexia:

- Genetic/hereditary factors (Gilger 2008; Stein 2017) – it is estimated that if one of the parents has dyslexia, there is around a four-to-one chance of the children also experiencing dyslexia in some form.

- Sequencing difficulties in carrying out tasks and gaining automaticity in these tasks (Fawcett and Nicolson 2008) – 'automaticity' means being able to carry out a task automatically, without too much forethought or thinking. For example, when we as adults read a newspaper or drive a car, or go about daily chores, we tend to do these automatically – this is because we have already gone through the learning process, and now have automaticity in these tasks. There is evidence that children with dyslexia can take longer to achieve automaticity in a number of tasks, including reading, writing and spelling.

- Processing speed difficulties (Norton and Wolf 2012) – this means that the person would take longer to carry out a task, and will therefore need more time. Later in school, this would have implications for exams, and additional time might be needed.

- Working memory difficulties (Gathercole 2018; Jeffries and Everatt 2004) – this is an important factor, as it means that instructions will probably need to be repeated. Parents often note this quite early on, and usually refer to this as one of the reasons for an assessment.

- Difficulties with phonological and language development (Snowling 2017) – this is commented on a great deal in later chapters, because it is an important prerequisite for reading, and especially important for beginning readers.

- Overlap with other Specific Learning Difficulties (SpLDs) (Bishop and Snowling 2004; Fawcett 2017; Wolf and Berninger 2015) – this is referred to in later chapters. It relates to the overlap that might exist between different difficulties – for example, as well as dyslexia there can be difficulties relating to dyspraxia (co-ordination difficulties), dysgraphia (handwriting and fine motor difficulties) or dyscalculia (significant number difficulties). It is believed that an overlap is the norm rather than the exception.

- Lowered literacy achievement (Joshi and Aaron 2008; Rose 2009) – this is also one of the main 'warning signs', and can often be the reason for an assessment. Parents, as well as teachers, can often spot this quite early. It might be more difficult for parents if it is their first child. Although parents generally do appreciate that children develop at different rates, and are often careful about making comparisons, they often notice if a child is finding the initial stages of reading more difficult, or if the child seems to be taking a different approach to learning. They also notice if their child is having difficulty in retaining letters and sounds, and requires a lot of repetition.

The above list highlights the range of factors that can be associated with dyslexia. Not everyone diagnosed with dyslexia will show all of those characteristics, but most are likely to show persistent challenges with literacy in some form.

It is important that children with dyslexia are identified early, and that proactive approaches are put in place. This can prevent or minimise the potentially damaging and enduring impact of dyslexia. Early identification does not necessarily mean early labelling. We advocate that identifying the barriers to learning and the child's specific learning needs should take precedence over labelling in very young children. We do, however, suggest in this book that acknowledging and using the term 'dyslexia' is important for all concerned – child, school and parents.

Definition

We see dyslexia in the following way:

> Dyslexia is a processing difference, often characterised by difficulties in literacy acquisition affecting reading, writing and spelling. It can also have an impact on cognitive processes such as memory, speed of processing, time management, co-ordination and automaticity. There may be visual and/or phonological challenges, and there are usually some discrepancies in educational performance.

It is important to recognise the strengths that can also form part of a dyslexic profile, and that children may need support to be able to utilise or to demonstrate these strengths. There will invariably be individual differences and individual variation, and it is therefore important to consider individual learning preferences as well as the education and work context when planning and implementing interventions and accommodations.

This definition highlights processing differences, as well as the cognitive challenges such as memory, organisation and processing speed.

Individual differences

It is important to recognise that children and young people with dyslexia are individuals, and their particular learning preferences and individual differences need to be acknowledged. Not all children and adults with dyslexia will have the same profile, although they may meet the criteria for dyslexia. Some of the common difficulties relate to the following.

Phonological processing

There is substantial evidence that the acquisition of phonological skills is crucial for successful reading, and that difficulties in acquiring phonological skills are fundamental in dyslexia (Vellutino *et al.* 2004; Snowling 2017). From this viewpoint, early phonological training is recommended; see:

www.beatingdyslexia.com/phonological-disorder.html

Cognitive skills

'Cognition' is the term used to describe the processes of learning and thinking that take place when any task is being carried out. This can relate to how information is taken in – visual, auditory (listening), tactile (touch) and kinaesthetic (experience). It can also relate to how the learner understands the information, and how he or she demonstrates that understanding (e.g. orally or in writing). Children with dyslexia can show difficulties at any of these stages, and this has implications for teaching and learning.

The child's cognitive preferences and preferences for learning will also have implications for parents. Understanding this can help parents understand why their child is not picking up and retaining information, even though he or she seems bright in other areas.

Cognitive skills can include phonological processing as well as memory, processing speed (both discussed in more detail below), and other factors relating to learning.

Literacy difficulties
Phonological difficulties

This will mean the child will have problems decoding new words, and this will have an impact on reading fluency, reading accuracy and reading comprehension. It is important that all three are considered – accuracy, fluency and comprehension. Written expression, which includes spelling, is also a key factor in dyslexia. In *DSM-5* (*Diagnostic and Statistical Manual of Mental Disorders*),[1] written expression is a

---

1   *DSM-5* is the manual used by clinicians and researchers to diagnose and classify mental disorders. The American Psychiatric Association (APA) published *DSM-5* in 2013, at the end of a 14-year revision process.

separate category (315.2) but still comes under the same umbrella label as 'dyslexia (impairment in reading) – specific learning disorder'.

Difficulty decoding words

This involves learning words and letters, as well as a difficulty with phonics (sounds). Word attack skills (the strategies used by the reader to tackle an unfamiliar word) are important for reading. They are needed when we come across new or unfamiliar words in text. Even words that a child already knows may have to be decoded, because he or she might not have automaticity in reading that particular word.

Reluctance to read

This can be a sign that the child is experiencing difficulties with reading, and this needs to be investigated further. Parents can note this quite early on and may well be aware of this before the school.

Difficulties with spelling

It may take the child a long time to learn spellings, and then they can be easily forgotten. Some children can do quite well in spelling tests because they work hard to revise for them, then they find they cannot consistently remember the same words in everyday use. This can cause frustration and result in low self-esteem, and perhaps a reluctance to write.

Handwriting

Not all children with dyslexia will have handwriting difficulties, but many will and this needs to be addressed. Handwriting difficulties can have an impact on expressive writing, and for that reason children might show a reluctance to write.

Reversal of letters or numbers

This can be seen in some children, but is not a key identification factor.

Confusion with signs and symbols in numeracy

These could include, for example, misreading the operator (for example, carrying out a minus sum instead of a plus sum), or difficulties with worded questions. It is quite often the language of maths that causes problems, and children with these difficulties will need close monitoring when doing maths problems.

Processing difficulties

Poor memory

This is often a sign of dyslexia, although not all children with dyslexia will have a poor memory. There are, broadly, three categories of memory – short-term memory, working memory and long-term memory. Short-term memory is a very temporary store that would be used, for example, when we repeat a telephone number, or when we hold information long enough to note it down. If we have to carry out a task using information in our heads, we are using working memory. This could include doing mental arithmetic, or taking notes that summarise what is being said. Long-term memory is more akin to a filing cabinet – if we know where we have stored the information, we can later retrieve it. This is important for revision.

Children with dyslexia may have a working memory that does not match their reasoning ability. That is, they do not always retain every piece of information for long enough to process it as well as they might. Working memory difficulties can mean that more repetition or practice is needed to store information in long-term memory.

Working memory difficulties can also be associated with a delay in retrieving information from long-term memory. So, a child might know the information but be unable to recall it without prompts. The key thing is to identify which prompts are the most effective! The following characteristics can be seen in the child with working memory difficulties:

- **Difficulty remembering letters of the alphabet** – this is very often noted in young children with dyslexia.

- **Listening to and following instructions** – this can often be mistaken for attention difficulties, but in fact the main problem can be auditory processing or working memory difficulties and dyslexia.

- **Following the sequence in a story** – children with dyslexia may be able to tell you some of the points about a story, but they might provide you with fairly random pieces of information. They can often have a difficulty with the order of the story.

- **Forgetfulness** – this would be more than the occasional instance of forgetfulness, but something that is obvious most of the time.

- **Concentration** – when a task is very challenging for children, it becomes quite difficult for them to maintain concentration. This can often be confused with attention difficulties.

- **Losing and misplacing items** – many children do this, but it can be a feature of dyslexia all the way through school. It can be particularly noted in later stages of education, where the student has to remember quite a number of different items for different subjects. It can also be a factor at other stages too, such as pre-school and the early stages of education.

- **Poor organisation of materials** – difficulties with organisation can be an issue for children with dyslexia. Often, they will have a lot of materials to work with at any one time, and materials might need to be arranged and organised.

- **Remembering the routines of the class and the school** – this can be quite a challenge for children with dyslexia, and can make them feel quite inadequate at times. It is important to help children devise strategies to deal with this.

Processing speed difficulties

Breznitz (2008) suggests that dyslexia is caused by gaps in the speed of processing within and between the various elements in the word-decoding process. Processing speed is usually one of the more readily identifiable characteristics of dyslexia; more information on this is available at:

> www.dyslexicadvantage.org/understanding-processing-speed-and-dyslexia

Processing speed can also be seen with reaction time, as well as the time taken to carry out a task. This tends to be one of the persistent indicators of dyslexia, and can have an impact all the way through school. It is important to note that difficulties in processing speed can put an extra burden on working memory.

Co-ordination difficulties

- **Tasks that require fine-motor skills** such as tying shoelaces – difficulties here can be quite common among young children with dyslexia, and they may have difficulties with other fine motor activities such as tracing and colouring in pictures. We find that obtaining information from parents on pre-school milestones can be useful. As they progress through school, children with co-ordination difficulties might have problems forming letters and words, and/or producing joined handwriting. Handwriting might be slow and/or difficult to read.

- **Gross motor skills difficulties** (for example, bumping into tables and chairs, difficulties throwing or catching a ball) – not all children with dyslexia will have these difficulties, but it is something to look out for and can be fairly easy to spot in the younger child. Significant difficulties with gross motor skills can point towards dyspraxia (see Appendix 2 for a definition).

  Dyspraxia is essentially a difficulty with co-ordination and organisation, and the child with dyspraxia may be seen as being quite clumsy and perhaps even accident-prone, as he or she may trip and fall easily. Like dyslexia, dyspraxia can be seen as a learning difference, and it has a broad range of characteristics. The term dyspraxia is used interchangeably with DCD (Developmental Co-ordination Disorder). According to *DSM-5*, for a diagnosis of dyspraxia the child must have difficulty in acquiring and using co-ordinated motor skills, and these should be substantially below what is expected for his or her chronological age. There may also be speech difficulties, but not always. A diagnosis of dyspraxia usually involves a number of professionals, including an occupational therapist and psychologist, and perhaps other health professionals and speech and language therapists.

Family and developmental background

- Incidence of dyslexic difficulties in the family – Molfese *et al.* (2008) indicate that there is a large body of research showing that children are at risk if there is a family history of dyslexia (see also Francks, MacPhil and Monaco 2002; Stein 2014).

- Speech and language development – for example, poor discrimination of sounds, habitually using the wrong word and sequencing difficulties. The child might have difficulty understanding the meaning of concepts such as 'more/less', 'same/different' or 'before/after'.

Behavioural and emotional indicators

- **Self-esteem** – there can be an impact on self-esteem as the child develops and becomes more aware of his or her difficulties, and is able to compare his or her performances with others.

- **Motivation** – if children fail at a task, they can naturally become reluctant to keep on trying. This is what often happens with children who are dyslexic and have difficulties with reading. They can become less motivated to read, and this can generalise to other areas in school. Some children can show great creativity in their ways of avoiding tasks they find difficult, or where they cannot show their full abilities.

- **Signs of not enjoying school** – this can also be a factor that needs to be investigated; in this case, it is best to find out what the child does enjoy, and to try to highlight and develop that activity. If he or she is not enjoying reading, for example, then this needs to be investigated further, and the parents should make an appointment to discuss this with the school.

- **Reluctance to go to school** – this can be a sign that all is not well for whatever reason. This needs to be investigated, and it can happen because the child is experiencing a lot of difficulties in the work being done in class. This needs to be investigated before it becomes the main problem!

Obtaining an assessment

This chapter has indicated the range of difficulties associated with dyslexia, and highlighted that dyslexia is not a single entity, but includes a variety of characteristics. These indicators may well be noted by parents as well as teachers. Just as there is no one single gene that can cause dyslexia, there is not one single test that can identify it. This is made clear in the following chapters, and it underlines the importance of a full assessment being carried out using a variety of tests and other assessment procedures.

It may be necessary for parents to initiate the assessment, although often the school will pick up any discrepancies in the child's profile quite early on. If this does not happen and the parent suspects dyslexia, then a meeting with the school is necessary as a matter of priority. Ideally, the school is the first port of call for the parent who is concerned about his or her child. Alternatively, the parent can initiate an assessment with a registered independent practitioner psychologist who can use a battery of tests. Details of this procedure and the tests that can be used are discussed in later chapters of this book.

In the UK, the Health and Care Professions Council (HCPC) displays a list of practising psychologists who are HCPC-registered at their website:

www.hcpc-uk.org

Some local dyslexia organisations may have a list of practising psychologists in their geographical area. However, as indicated above, any concerns held by parents should be first discussed with the school.

In the UK, there is also a growing number of specialist teacher assessors – teachers who have undergone specialist training in assessment. Some of these are independent specialists who can also be consulted privately. The main difference from practitioner psychologists is that specialist teachers are not eligible to use 'closed' tests such as the Wechsler Intelligence Scale (please see Appendix 1 for a description of assessment tests). However, they are able to access other ability tests such as the Wide Range Intelligence Tests (WRIT), as long as they have qualified teaching status, and a further postgraduate diploma or Masters qualification. This qualification would need to be in SEN (Special Educational Needs), SpLD, or a relevant field. For more information see:

www.pearsonclinical.co.uk/information/qualificationcodes.
aspx#CL2R

Specialist teacher assessors can access a vast range of attainment tests, and can therefore provide a full and detailed report with appropriate recommendations based on the findings from the assessment.

Summary

We have noted the wide range of factors associated with dyslexia in this chapter, and this demonstrates the need for a comprehensive assessment. This opening chapter has mentioned the need for early identification, and for clearly identifying the specific learning needs of young children with dyslexia. It is important for parents and teachers to see dyslexia in a broader way, and not to focus on a narrow or unitary factor.

It is important to realise that not all children with dyslexia will have the same profile, and this means that not all will warrant the same intervention. For that reason, parents need to seek advice before buying expensive products or commercially advertised treatments. Often, the school can provide this advice, but there are other useful resources, such as local and national dyslexia associations – for example, in the UK we have the British Dyslexia Association, the Helen Arkell Centre and Dyslexia Scotland, and in the USA there are organisations such as the International Dyslexia Association (see Appendix 3 for details of these organisations). If the assessment is carried out privately, then the psychologist or specialist teacher assessor can recommend appropriate programmes and strategies based on the child's individual profile.

The following chapters will develop some of the points mentioned here, and discuss the purpose and practice of an assessment and the importance of recommendations that can help the young person with dyslexia enjoy a successful educational experience.

Chapter 2

Being Dyslexic

Every dyslexic person will have a different story, a different profile of abilities and difficulties, and a different way of dealing with them. We have found, though, over the course of many years of working with dyslexic people, that certain themes do emerge. We have also seen these same themes in a number of books, blogs and videos that describe being dyslexic, from the dyslexic person's point of view. These are listed at the end of this chapter. Please note that quotations from the Dyslexia Scotland book retain the spelling and grammar of the original, because it seemed important to hear people's stories from the heart. This chapter will be of great interest to parents, and we hope it can give them hope and support, and help them to see the positive side of dyslexia, as well as the challenges that might be experienced by their child.

We would also like to stress the importance of keeping a good level of communication with your child, to get his or her particular views. Of course, children (and their parents) might not always want to discuss this, but it is important that they know that children can talk about their feelings of being dyslexic, when the time is right for them. Certainly, one of the themes that recurs in Rooke's (2018) interviews is that dyslexia is not something that we can see:

> 'Dyslexia for me is like having a superpower. People can see me but they don't understand how I do what I do.' (Rooke 2018, p.29)

This means that we really do need to try to find out as much as we can about how it is affecting each individual child.

It is not surprising to know that, for many people, the experience of being dyslexic can be negative – especially at the stage when they and the people surrounding them don't yet really understand what is going on. Fortunately, there are so many positive aspects and experiences. We will talk about these, and how they can help to improve outcomes for the child.

Some potential negative experiences of being dyslexic

The potential downsides of being dyslexic are discussed below, and can be seen in terms of:

- the child's self-esteem
- the extra effort that can be involved in keeping up with class work
- relationships with peers, teachers and parents
- having the right type and level of support.

Self-esteem

Often, the first thing that people will say when they find that they are dyslexic is that they are relieved to know that they are not 'stupid'. They describe periods of doubting themselves, when they look around at other people in their class who seem to be able to manage things more easily. They can feel angry or frustrated with themselves. Sometimes, they describe periods of feeling worthless, ashamed or embarrassed:

> 'I hated school becuse I could not grasp the concept of what the Teachers were trying to teach. I was always putting my self down and had the feelings of worthlessness believing that I was thick, stupid. I was so unhappy and ashamed as well as embarrassed. So many feelings on the shoulders of a young child.' (Dyslexia Scotland 2011, p.17)

> 'I have asked the question "why?" since I was four years old! Why can other people do this and I can't?' (Reid and Kirk 2001, p.159)

Brian Conley, entertainer, actor and singer, describes how, in his early years at school, he felt as if he came from another planet. Former Scottish rugby player Kenny Logan describes anxiety that made him feel as if he had a constant ache inside him (Rooke 2016).

Sometimes, children have the feeling that they should be able to keep up – because they know that they have the ability – but that there seems to be something stopping them, and this means there must be something wrong with them. When we talk about these things, we would always be keen to point out that the difficulty can be more to do with the way the child is being asked to do something (for example, being given a lot of verbal instructions all at once) or to do with the way the child has to demonstrate his or her knowledge (for example, having to write it down in full sentences rather than using bullet points, or better still talking through the answers). We would also always stress the positive aspects of the child's profile and abilities.

Extra effort in keeping up with class work

Dyslexic pupils often tell us about the sheer amount of work that they have to do to keep up with class during the day. It can be hard to keep up the level of effort required, and they might find that at times they get completely lost. This is quite likely to happen when they are tired, hungry or thirsty. Children can be exhausted – and sometimes irritable – when they get home, and they don't always feel like doing homework.

> 'I wanted so much to learn and I tried very hard... I had to stand up in class and read aloud, I always stuttered and eventually through sheer frustration lost control, scattered the objects on my desk and ran out of the room in tears.' (Reid and Kirk 2001, p.159)

> 'I have horrible memories of having questions fired at me, and not being fast enough.' (Guise interview notes)

Relationships with peers, teachers and parents

One of the difficulties that dyslexic children often talk about is the fact that their extra efforts to keep up, and to produce good work, can go unnoticed. Of course, it is not always easy for the outsider to see how much a child is trying to concentrate when on the surface it looks like the opposite – as if he or she is daydreaming or 'zoning out'. From the child's point of view, though, this can feel very unfair.

> 'In spite of my enormous efforts to impress teachers and other pupils, my teachers thought I wasn't making an effort.' (Dyslexia Scotland 2011, p.90)

> 'I was told that I was slapdash, and that I should slow down and pay more attention to detail... I had a lot of fear in me academically.' (Guise interview notes)

It is particularly hard when the teacher's or parent's disapproval is made obvious to others – to the child's peer group. Other children can be quite cruel to a child who seems in some way different, and who doesn't seem to fit in. This can lead to a number of reactions. Some children withdraw and do their best not to be noticed. Unfortunately, by doing this they can miss out on opportunities for support. Sometimes children do the opposite and will try to win over their peers by being the 'class clown', or by doing all they can to avoid doing tasks that might demonstrate their weaknesses. TV motorcycle adventurer Charley Boorman describes getting into terrible trouble at school, and recognising this pattern of behaviour in other dyslexic children (Rooke 2016).

Dyslexic children sometimes find it hard when they get poor results compared with others in their friendship groups. They can find that this affects their relationships with their close peers; it can be hard not to become jealous, or resentful, at times:

> 'I have a very clever group of friends and I tried to do what everyone else was doing to make myself feel better inside… Everyone was saying how hard the work was and how much they hated revising and how they did badly in the exams and then they all opened their envelopes on results day and got A stars. I thought "you fibbers". I opened mine and everything I hoped for had been taken from me.' (Rooke 2018, pp.102–103)

Having the right type and level of support

When we speak to dyslexic pupils, or adults who are talking about their time at school, they often feel that they have not had the right type and level of support for their needs. There are many reasons for this. Sometimes, people will admit that they have rejected offers of help because they did not want to be seen as different from their friends.

The following examples highlight the importance of an assessment. It can be the trigger for a smoother and more appropriate path for the individual, and can help to relieve some of the stressors that can accompany dyslexia. We find that parents in particular are usually relieved and can be quite emotional during the feedback when a diagnosis is presented. Assessment therefore can be the key ingredient for eventual success. The assessment also promotes self-advocacy, and this is crucial for the young person with dyslexia, particularly as he or she advances further up the school and also in further and higher education and the workplace! Self-advocacy can stem from self-knowledge, and the assessment can provide the individual with this self-knowledge.

> 'It took 25 years before I could find the words to write about dyslexia. Even now there's a sense of embarrassment of drawing attention to it. It's a worry about making a fuss, about being measured against other people in greater need but perhaps above all a burning and lasting sense that it's somehow an excuse for laziness and stupidity.' (Dyslexia Scotland 2011, p.49)

Sometimes this extends to exam accommodations – a pupil might be recommended extra time, or access to a computer, but not want to take up this opportunity. Scottish footballer Steven Naismith wrote that he did not want to be taken out of class, but his parents forced him to have support. He is now 100 per cent pleased that he did, and that he had the extra time he needed in exams (Rooke 2016).

In our experience, even when people know about dyslexia, they do not always understand all of the implications. They might be aware of possible difficulties with reading or spelling, and aspects of writing. However, they might not realise that the difficulties that underlie dyslexia can cause problems in other areas. For example, it can be very hard to take notes from the board, or when someone is talking. Retaining a list of verbal instructions can be very difficult. The bigger and less structured the task is, the more challenging it can be. Typically, dyslexic pupils will find it hard to produce extended written work that is well structured and that is free of grammatical errors.

The dyslexic pupil sometimes feels unsupported because these areas are not addressed. We find that this is often the case in later stages of education, because the demands are greater, and subject-specialist teachers do not always have the same background in literacy development as teachers working in the early stages of education. Of course, the dyslexic pupil might not be aware of these aspects of dyslexia either, but they can still feel that it seems that their needs are not being fully addressed.

For those dyslexic pupils with very high aptitude, it can seem that help is not well targeted to their needs. These pupils can express frustration at having to spend time in support, working on things that they find too easy, when what might work better for them is to be given the time and opportunity to show what they are capable of. This might involve giving fewer examples of a new concept to be learnt, and effectively more time to complete these examples. It can involve access to technologies, or more generic study skills support, so that the pupil can work independently.

Some positive experiences of being dyslexic

It is so important to stress the positive aspects of dyslexia, and the strategies that can be used by children to improve their self-esteem and their performance. The themes that emerge here are:

- creativity and thinking 'outside the box'
- problem-solving skills and resourcefulness
- self-knowledge
- support and understanding from others
- role models
- advocacy.

Creativity and thinking 'outside the box'

Many people who are dyslexic have come to value the different perspective that they can have, compared to most others. This theme comes out strongly in Rooke's (2016) *Creative, Successful, Dyslexic* book. David Bailey, the world-renowned photographer, writes that he is glad that he is dyslexic. He stands out from others who might be looking at the same thing, because he thinks differently, and literally sees things differently. Eddie Izzard is an award-winning comedian and actor who feels that being dyslexic means that he makes 'sideways' and unusual connections between things, and this is a key part of his creativity. Dyslexia can be an asset in business – Sir Richard Branson describes it as his 'greatest strength'. He has become adept at simplifying things, focusing on the areas he is good at and delegating in areas of weakness.

In feedback discussions, we often stress the fact that creativity is such a hard thing to teach, so if it comes naturally that is a wonderful thing. It is always good when children already have a sense of what a rare talent they have:

'I am an eleven-year-old dyslexic boy and although when I was younger dyslexia got the better of me I now see it as a gift, the power to see the world in a different dimention.' (Dyslexia Scotland 2011, p.197)

'I feel like my brain is created in the way no one else is. I think of a brain being shot by a lightning bolt of smartness.' (Rooke 2018, p.25)

Problem-solving skills and resourcefulness

Sometimes dyslexic people do not see themselves as creative in the artistic sense, but nevertheless they have developed the ability to problem-solve. This could be a feature of dyslexia. It could equally be the result of always having to think of new or different ways to tackle things that other people might find more straightforward. Certainly, dyslexic people are often very resourceful in devising strategies to help them to achieve their potential. Some people have described this in terms of an ultimately positive outcome to negative experiences:

'The Head told me I would go nowhere unless I improved drastically. Perhaps that is the reason why I forced myself to go as far as I could in my career.' (Reid and Kirk 2001, p.157)

Some of the children in Rooke's (2018) interviews point out that it is really important to work harder, and not to use dyslexia as an excuse to avoid things – because this would take away an opportunity for growth:

'The best thing for me about dyslexia is that I have to try harder. People who think they are good at things might choose the easiest route, but even the easiest thing is quite difficult for me. Determination keeps me learning. I never give up. I always keep trying.' (Rooke 2018, p.170)

Theo Paphitis, a former BBC *Dragon's Den* judge, wrote that all of the many struggles that he had at school taught him to look at a situation, figure out what was going wrong, and think of a solution to fix it.

Self-knowledge

We find in working with dyslexic people that they have often developed a keen awareness of what works for them, in terms of how they learn and how they can demonstrate their knowledge. Finding out that they are dyslexic is often a very positive experience. One young boy describes how happy he was to find out that there was a reason for his difficulties:

> 'When I was told I was dyslexic everything clicked. It explains who I am and I felt relieved that I know about it and what it means for me.' (Rooke 2018, p.162)

We have both taught a range of students, and have found that those who might not ever have struggled academically can find that they seem to hit a wall when things do become difficult. So, dyslexic students can have a better-developed self-knowledge. This is a crucial element of independent learning. It should be the ultimate aim for any teacher or parent that the child can transfer their strategies and skills to new contexts, and new environments.

Support and understanding from others

Some of the children in Rooke's (2018) interviews spoke about the advantage of realising how kind and helpful other people can be:

> 'A lot of my friends help me with words that I'm struggling with. In fact, being dyslexic has shown me how nice people are. My friends are interested in what I do. My friends say I'm better than them at things and I say it's not that I'm better, it's that we're all different... We help each other.' (Rooke 2018, p.119)

In nearly all of the positive stories of dyslexia, people will mention the value of support and understanding from siblings, peers, parents and teachers:

> 'If it was not for some of the amazing teachers I have been lucky enough to have had, my education would have turned out so very differently. Eventually with their kindness, support, patient and laughter, together we found small solutions I was able to apply on my own... Living with dyslexia for me has been a big adventure,

which seemed in the beginning to be something I was going to struggle to overcome.' (Dyslexia Scotland 2011, p.12)

'Grammar school was potentially tough but I soon learnt to use coping strategies and got considerable support from my English teacher who gave me individual support at lunchtimes... I have been fortunate in the support from my family and friends.' (Reid and Kirk 2001, p.166)

Richard Rogers, an award-winning architect who worked on the Pompidou Centre in Paris, wrote that his parents loved and supported him and always encouraged him to aim high. As he sees it, this is the best thing a parent can do, and it costs nothing (Rooke 2016).

Of course, it is important that the dyslexic child feels able to ask for, and to accept, help and support. Kenny Logan's advice to children is that he wished that he had been brave enough as a child to admit how hard things were for him at school (Rooke 2016).

Role models

Often, someone else in the family is dyslexic, and this can be very helpful because that person might be able to understand some of the difficulties faced by the child. If a parent or older sibling is dyslexic, then often he or she is seen as a role model. A sense of humour can also go a long way to help defuse difficulties:

'I am pleased my Dad has dyslexia as this makes us laugh.' (Dyslexia Scotland 2011, p.4)

Advocacy

If people who are dyslexic are to receive the support they need, they will often have to negotiate this themselves, and certainly in the later stages of their education. This is because their learning needs will change over time and in relation to the type of work they are doing. In her interviews with dyslexic children, Rooke (2018) found that many of them also wanted to help other dyslexic children, and often they said they would like to be teachers:

'I'm going to study primary school teaching at university. I want to become a primary school teacher and would like to help people when they're little to figure out all the big stuff like reading and writing. I want to make it fun and easier for them.' (Rooke 2018, p.160)

People with dyslexia can certainly bring a very valuable insight to the process of teaching and learning. Caring about others has been described by some children as one of the possible effects of having had to struggle with dyslexia.

Interestingly, Benjamin Zephaniah – who describes himself as a poet, writer, lyricist, musician and troublemaker – writes that if people do not understand dyslexia, it is up to them to learn about it (and not up to the dyslexic person to change his or her way of learning) (Rooke 2016). We would add that people who are not dyslexic might be very willing to help, but they might well need a few pointers!

We hope that this chapter has provided some pointers in terms of some of the experiences described by people who are dyslexic. As noted earlier, children and parents do not always have the inclination, or the words, to express their feelings about dyslexia. Other children's experiences can be used as a starting point for good communication about being dyslexic.

Useful resources

Books

Campbell, A. (2009) *A Dyslexic Writes: An Essay on Dyslexia – A Conundrum of Conundrums*. Farnham: Helen Arkell Dyslexia Centre.

Dyslexia Scotland (2011) *Dyslexia and Us: A Collection of Personal Stories*. Stirling: Dyslexia Scotland.

Kurnoff, S. (2000) *The Human Side of Dyslexia: 142 Interviews with Real People Telling Real Stories*. Monterey, CA: London Universal.

Reid, G. and Kirk, J. (2001) *Dyslexia in Adults: Education and Employment*. Chichester: Wiley.

Rooke, M. (2016) *Creative, Successful, Dyslexic: 23 High Achievers Share their Stories*. London: Jessica Kingsley Publishers.

Rooke, M. (2018) *Dyslexia Is My Superpower (Most of the Time)*. London: Jessica Kingsley Publishers.

Websites

Children's blogs about being dyslexic: https://dyslexia-assist.org.uk/blogs/kids-blogs

Discussion of the film *Dyslexia – The Big Picture*: www.youtube.com/watch?v=Dg_ZCgeWXko

Documentary with actress Kara Tointon: www.youtube.com/watch?v=L7cfD0PMV84

I Am Dyslexic, a documentary for school-aged children (12 years and above) about dyslexia, by adults who identify as dyslexic: https://youtu.be/FDymP3VAZ8o

Inspirational quotes from inspirational people: www.facebook.com/madeby dyslexia/videos/994311874073805

Keira Knightley OBE – Made By Dyslexia Interview: www.youtube.com/ watch?v=OLb6ehPPc4E

Chapter 3

The Purpose of an Assessment

Why is an assessment important, and is it necessary? We find many parents and teachers, quite rightly, ask these questions, particularly if an independent assessment is requested. An independent assessment takes place usually outwith the school, but this is not always the case, and the school can sometimes arrange things so that the assessment takes place at school. This has the advantage that feedback can sometimes be given to the teacher (or teachers) and the parents at the same time. This emphasises the point made in the previous chapter that communication between all parties involved is a crucial aspect of an assessment.

Schools will often have their own procedures for assessing children, but when the child is not responding – despite appropriate intervention – a further, detailed assessment may be requested using an independent, registered psychologist, or a specialist teacher. If the problem seems to be speech-orientated, a speech and language specialist may be referred to. If it is more an issue with co-ordination and movement, then an occupational therapist referral may be appropriate.

There may therefore be a number of different reasons why an assessment is required, but there are usually some common factors.

Reasons for school and independent assessments

- The assessment may be used for **diagnostic** purposes – that is, to diagnose if there is an issue, and to identify whether the difficulties meet the criteria for dyslexia, or some other SpLD.

- The assessment may be used as a **predictive** tool, to obtain information that can help the teacher predict how the child will cope with particular aspects of the curriculum. Used in this way, however, the information from the assessment may in fact be misused; it may lead to unnecessary curricular restrictions being placed on the child. This is one of the 'misuses' of IQ tests, since the case may arise where a child assessed as having a low IQ is disadvantaged in terms of curricular access and expectation, and, of course, this should be avoided at all costs.

- The assessment may be used in a **'normative'** way, by comparing the child with his or her peers. Some caution should be applied here, as the school may have a higher-than-average ability–achievement ratio. Nevertheless, it may still be useful to obtain some kind of data on how the child is progressing in relation to others in the same age range.

- If the child has already been assessed, then further assessment can contribute to **monitoring and review**. This is an important element of any assessment, since it can help to measure the impact of teaching. Schools will usually prefer ongoing assessment. This is very important as progress sheets can be obtained in termly/semester reports.

- Assessment should be **linked to teaching**. There should be a prescriptive element to assessment, and it should **provide suggestions for teaching approaches or programmes**. This is a very important element in all assessments, but particularly independent assessments, as often this type of assessment can lend itself to a wider view of teaching and learning, and can suggest approaches in addition to those used in the school.

The importance of feedback

Feedback following the assessment is very important, and can in itself justify the need for the assessment. If there is a feeling that the child may have dyslexic difficulties, and the assessment is being conducted to discover if this is indeed the case, then feeding back this information, particularly to the parents, is essential. If the difficulties are to be effectively tackled, then it is important that the school, parents and the child should be working collaboratively.

Feedback can take a number of forms. These include:

- **School meetings** – these are perhaps the most effective form of feedback, because everyone involved is likely to be present. At this session, the assessor will discuss what type of assessment was carried out, and the tests that were used. The results of the assessment will be indicated, and perhaps how some of the results compare to others in the pupil's age range. Very importantly, the next steps will be indicated, and the type of teaching and learning approaches that should be used in the light of the assessment.

The importance of this type of meeting is that school assessments may be multi-disciplinary, which means that a number of professionals can be involved, including the teacher, school management, the psychologist and the specialist teacher, and any others involved, including the parents. This brings everyone together, and helps to form unity and agreement in what needs to be done following the assessment.

- **Meeting with the independent assessor** – this is likely to be with the psychologist, specialist teacher assessor or other professionals, who may have been involved in the assessment. This can be particularly useful for parents, as it is usually a one-to-one meeting, and may be less intimidating than a large school meeting. But if this meeting is outwith the school, the parents will still need to take the report to the school and discuss it there. It may, however, be possible for the independent assessor to accompany the parent to a school meeting.

- **The written report** – this is an important part of the assessment. The report is usually a formal, written document that can be retained in the school records if the parents wish that. The details of the report are discussed in the next chapter, but in general the report should detail all the tests that were used and the results, with explanations of what the results mean and implications of the results for learning and for classroom practice. A diagnosis, if appropriate, will also be provided. An important part of the report is the recommendations section, and this should be helpful for the parents and for the school.

- **Review meeting** – a period of time after the initial assessment, a review meeting should be held. In some situations, for example when an Individual Education Plan (IEP) or its equivalent (for example, an Individualized Education Program in the USA) has been written, a review is built in, and sometimes it is statutory. In any case, it is good practice to review progress, particularly if a new programme or approach has been implemented.

What should an assessment provide?

An assessment should provide some or all of the following:

- **An indication of the learner's strengths and weaknesses, or learning preferences** – it is important to look at strengths as well as the difficulties, and to consider the way the child learns best. This is because it can provide a more positive overtone to the assessment, but additionally it is a good idea to start a lesson or a new piece of learning by utilising the learner's stronger areas.

- **An indication of the learner's current level of performance in attainments** – this is important, as it can provide a baseline for deciding which resources or approaches might work best. It can also help to set achievement targets.

- **An explanation for the learner's level of progress** – this would be helpful to obtain, as it may be that a different approach needs to be tried and/or that expectations need to be adjusted.

- **Information on the nature of the difficulties the child is experiencing** – it is very likely that the school and the parents will know that the child has, for example, a reading difficulty, but they will want to know why, and what type of difficulty. An identification of the learner's performances and errors in reading, writing and spelling may show a distinctive pattern, and this can help to identify the way forward in terms of resources and teaching.

- **Identification of specific areas of competence and skills** – this is important in terms of boosting the child's self-esteem, and in providing feedback to parents. It is good to know what the child *can* do, as well as what he or she cannot do.

- **An understanding of the student's learning preferences** – all children have different ways of learning, and therefore each will have learning preferences. It is useful to obtain some idea of these during the assessment or through the use of specific tests. This type of information can be useful for parents and teachers.

- **An indication of aspects of the curriculum that may interest and motivate the learner** – for a child with any type of learning issue, it is important to identify his or her interests and areas that can provide inspiration. Motivation is very important, as it is too easy for a child with difficulties to become demoralised. This is in fact a useful starting point when looking at a new programme or learning approach for the child.

- **Specific aspects of the curriculum that are challenging for the child** – this highlights the advantage of either school-based assessment, or obtaining information from the school if an independent assessment is to take place outwith the school. It is useful for the assessor to have an idea of what particular aspects of the school day are challenging for the learner. It may be that he or she does not fully understand the task, or the steps that are necessary to solve the problem. It is likely that not all aspects of the curriculum are challenging, so it is important to know which are the most troubling for the child. With this knowledge, the assessor is in a position to make suggestions that can help to minimise these challenges.

- **An indication of emotional and social development** – it is important not to overlook this. Quite often, the child's learning difficulties take prominence in an assessment and subsequent report. Emotional and social factors contribute to self-esteem, and the research clearly indicates that positive self-esteem is important for motivation and learning progress. The assessment should indicate strategies and perhaps resources that can boost self-esteem. This is important for parents, as well as for teachers.

- **Positive confirmation to parents and to teachers** – often the assessment confirms what is already suspected, but it can formalise and contextualise this. It may also explain why the child has experienced challenges, and also undo any misunderstandings that may already exist. For example, the two quotations below from parents highlight these points:

  'My son and myself have learnt so very much from the assessment and report, and I know this has given him an understanding of his work and certainly more confidence. This has had a very positive effect on him.'

  'With this report, any misunderstanding that there might have been in the past, describing him as "uncooperative", will now be remedied in a supportive way.'

The purpose of the assessment must be the first question to be asked – why should we have an assessment, and why now? This is crucial for the selection of the assessment approaches to be used, and the type of outcome expected from the assessment.

The assessment will provide a learning profile, and this can give an indication of the child's strengths and weaknesses, level of cognitive functioning and level of current performance in basic attainments. These factors are important, as there is much evidence connecting cognitive difficulties such as memory and processing speed to dyslexia, and the assessment should reveal whether there are difficulties in these areas.

The assessment will also provide diagnostic information, and will give suggestions about the learner's strategies and the nature of the difficulties, the type of tasks that may present difficulty, and some possible reasons for this difficulty.

For example, in a cognitive, working memory task involving digits that are reversed, one should be interested in *how* the learner achieved the correct or incorrect response. Identifying the strategies that the learners used can be an important piece of information, because the strategies can have an impact on learning.

Whatever the motivation for undertaking an assessment, it is important to have clear aims and objectives, and these should be known well before the assessment commences. It is also important to view assessment from the curriculum and learning perspectives, and not only within-child factors. Obtaining information from the school can help the assessor to work out the barriers to literacy and to learning that are experienced by the child.

Came and Reid (2008) suggest that when identifying the barriers to learning it is important to include: cognitive (learning skills), environmental (learning experience), and progress in basic attainments (literacy acquisition). This highlights the need not only to focus solely on the child, but to look at the task that is being presented, the expectations being placed on the learner, and the learner's readiness for the task. These aspects need to be taken up by the school.

A key aspect of this is the monitoring process, which must be based on actual curriculum attainments. The process can be extended to include details of the nature of the work within the curriculum that the child is finding challenging. For example, which letters does the child know and not know, which books can the child read fluently, and why should this be the case? Such an approach needs to view the child's class work in a comprehensive and detailed manner, otherwise it can become merely another type of checklist. Additionally, a degree of precision is needed to assist the teacher to see whether the child is achieving the targets. In order to do this, a sample of work is helpful, and should be taken from the actual work of the class.

The importance of this type of perspective is that the emphasis is on the barriers that prevent the child from meeting these targets, rather than identifying what the child cannot do. This is essentially a whole-school responsibility, as it is important that attitudes relating to progress and curriculum access are consistent throughout the school. Children who do have some difficulties and find aspects of the curriculum challenging can be very sensitive. For that reason, the assessment should also cater for aspects of self-esteem, social and emotional development, and motivation.

The assessment should conclude on a positive note, and it is heartening for the school and for the assessor to receive positive feedback from parents and teachers. Two such examples we received are shown below:

'Thank you so much. He is going to study architecture. Before the assessment, we would not have believed that possible.'

'She had little confidence before the assessment, and we knew she had a problem, but the assessment pinpointed the processing issues and overall the feedback gave her confidence, and she lifted her head and went for gold!'

Chapter 4

The Assessment Process

The assessment process can take different forms depending on what type of assessment is carried out. The different forms of assessment can include formal school-based assessment, independent assessment outwith school, psychologist in-school assessment and informal assessments, usually carried out at school often using observation/monitoring procedures, and school benchmarks for progression. Teachers will usually, as a matter of course, carry out informal assessments in order to check on the progress of the children in the class, but this may not in itself be sufficient for the identification of dyslexia and for developing an appropriate programme for the child with dyslexia. This type of assessment can sometimes identify children who are 'at risk' of dyslexia, but it does depend a great deal on the tests and screeners that are used.

This chapter will look at various procedures, including tests and screening instruments.

Irrespective of the type of assessment conducted, an assessment should consider all, or most, of the following:

- **Reasons for the assessment, and the anticipated expectations from the assessment** – there is always a reason for an assessment, whether it is part of the school's ongoing procedures to check progress, or to identify reasons why a child may not be progressing. It is important that parents in particular are aware of the reason prior to the assessment. Schools will usually be happy to give parents a reason why they want an assessment conducted – even if they are suggesting an independent assessment outside school, they will explain why they think this is necessary.

- **Consideration of the learner's cultural and linguistic background** – many schools are multi-cultural, and this needs to be considered throughout the assessment and particularly in the selection of tests that are to be used. Every effort should be made to ensure the assessment is 'culture-fair'.

- **Difficulties the child experienced in early years** – these would be incorporated into the early developmental background, but they can also include any pre-school factors. This information can be provided by parents, and, as indicated later in this chapter, this underlines the important role that parents play in assessment.

- **Information about previous tests and current and previous classroom performances** – it is important, whether the assessment takes place within the school or independently outside of school, that results of any previous tests are known. It is crucial that any trends, and progress, are noted. For example, it might be noted that the child has always shown low scores in processing speed, or low scores in memory tasks. Schools often use the same reading tests during the child's progression through the years, and this helps to see if the child is really progressing, and in which areas. For example, reading accuracy may be improving but his or her reading comprehension may have stagnated.

- **The class teacher's views on the child, and the strengths and difficulties shown by the child** – whether the assessment takes place within or outwith the school, it is important to obtain the class teacher's views. This can be taken for granted, but it is important that time is allowed for the class teacher to provide views and to expand on these with examples.

- **An individual learning profile for the student** – this can provide an outline of the student's strengths and weaknesses and provide pointers for action. This can also help to provide the information needed for an IEP (Individual Education Plan), or similar (for example, an Individualized Education Program in the USA).

- **Implications** – for the individual, the school or college, the parents and the family, and for subject and career choice, depending on the age of the student. This is important, as it relates the assessment to the student's educational needs – either at school or beyond school.

Checklists and screeners

There are a great number of checklists (of varying quality) in existence, but much of the information that is needed for a full assessment and diagnosis of the difficulties *cannot* be gathered from a basic checklist. Assessment is a dynamic process, and ideally this process should involve a range of strategies and tools, and be conducted in the learning context and over a period of time. This is why, if an assessment outwith the school is being arranged, then background and current information on school performance should be obtained.

Ideally, the person or team conducting the assessment should have information about the curriculum, the teaching approaches, the learning context and the learner's progress in school from early years. A checklist can provide pointers, however, for a follow-up assessment. For example, in the UK, the British Dyslexia Association have a useful primary school checklist:

> www.bdadyslexia.org.uk/common/ckeditor/filemanager/ userfiles/10_Primary_School_Dyslexia_Checklist.pdf

This consists of 38 questions that focus on strengths and difficulties. The checklist incorporates reading and reading speed, writing and copying information, following instructions, self-esteem and strengths, including problem-solving. What is striking about this checklist is that it incorporates a wide range of factors. This emphasises the fact that dyslexia should not be narrowly defined with only a few pointers, but in fact incorporates a broad range of signs and characteristics. A secondary school checklist is also available:

> www.bdadyslexia.org.uk/common/ckeditor/filemanager/ userfiles/Delegates_Pack_Secondary/Combined_checklist_ Secondary.pdf

In the USA, the International Dyslexia Association also has useful information and checklists and a useful factsheet on assessment for dyslexia:

> https://dyslexiaida.org/dyslexia-test

> https://dyslexiaida.org/dyslexia-assessment-what-is-it-and-how- can-it-help

The Helen Arkell Dyslexia Centre's checklist is also useful:

> www.helenarkell.org.uk/about-dyslexia/teachers-and-other- professionals/possible-indicators-of-dyslexia.php

The Dyslexia Screener Pack (age 5–16+ from GL Assessments) is one of the well-established suite of screeners:

www.glassessment.co.uk/products/dyslexia-screener-portfolio-and-guidance

The screener pack consists of a 'dyslexia screener', a 'dyslexia portfolio' and 'dyslexia guidance'. The screener consists of two tests covering three areas – ability, attainment and diagnostic. The portfolio is seen as a follow-up to the screener, and is aimed at those pupils where concern has been raised following administration of the initial screener. The portfolio provides a profile of strengths and weaknesses that can be translated into an individual teaching plan. The suite also contains a guidance handbook that contains advice and activities for use in the classroom or in small groups. The supporting website also contains advice and sample reports, including a sample report for a child who has been assessed as dyslexic, which is relevant to parents as well as the school:

www.gl-assessment.co.uk/support/dyslexia-support/sample-reports

www.gl-assessment.co.uk/media/1711/dyslexia-portfolio-report_parent.pdf

GL Assessment also provide the well-established Lucid suite of screeners for dyslexia:

www.gl-assessment.co.uk/products/lucid

These include the 'Lucid Exact', which looks at exam access arrangements; 'Lucid Rapid', which is a short, whole-class screener for dyslexia; 'LADS', which is a screener for the 15+ age range; 'CoPS', which is a dyslexia screener for young children; 'LASS', which identifies dyslexic tendencies and other learning needs; 'RECALL', which looks at speed and efficiency of working memory; and 'VISS', which looks at visual stress. There are also two booster tests – memory booster and comprehension booster. The website also contains a list of interesting and valuable factsheets on dyslexia.

SNAP, Special Educational Needs Assessment Profile (2018) offers online assessments designed to pinpoint specific learning and behavioural difficulties and targeted interventions based on the identification. SNAP includes information from home and school and follows the assess-plan-do-review stages set out in the SEND code of

Practice (2015). It provides interventions for 20 learning difficulties including 86 interventions for ages 4–6 and 134 interventions from ages 7–16.

https://www.hoddereducation.co.uk/snap

Some commercial reading programmes have developed websites with a bank of resources that can be easily obtained and used by parents, as well as schools. One such example is the 'Nessy' programme, which has information for 'parents and homeschoolers', reading and spelling programmes and strategies, a 'dyslexia quest screener', which is a game-based screening tool for dyslexia, and six games that involve memory, phonological awareness and processing speed:

www.nessy.com/uk/parents

www.nessy.com/uk/product/nessy-reading-spelling

www.nessy.com/uk/product/dyslexia-screening

What should an assessment consider?

Although screeners can be very useful, in many cases it will still be necessary to hold a full assessment for dyslexia. An assessment for dyslexia should consider four key aspects – the strengths, the difficulties, the range and variations of scores, and learning differences shown by the pupil. These factors, in addition to the background and ongoing school performance, can help to pinpoint whether the child has dyslexia or any other SpLD. Even if no diagnosis is made, then the assessment should still provide key information that can contribute to a learning profile. This information can help towards the development of a learning programme, and inform any other curriculum considerations that need to be made.

Strengths

It is important that the learner's strengths are noted in the assessment. Quite often, children with dyslexia can have visual strengths, and they may prefer to use visual strategies for reading. They might score quite highly in some of the visual activities in various tests (see Appendix 1 for a list of the visual skills assessed in the WISC 5 and the WAIS 4 cognitive tests).

In reading, the student may have a strength in comprehension but a difficulty in reading accuracy. Or the reverse may apply – he or she may read quite well, but have a difficulty in reading comprehension or in reading fluency (speed).

If the student's strengths are in social skills, sport or practical activities, these also need to be highlighted in the assessment and report. These can offer a 'lead-in' to the student's interests, and can help with motivation.

Difficulties

Children with dyslexia can experience a number of difficulties, and some of these were pointed out in Chapter 1. The main difficulty is usually related to the decoding or the encoding of print – that is, reading or spelling (or both). These difficulties can be due to challenges with phonological processing. There can be a difficulty in recognising and in retaining the sounds in words. They may have a difficulty in blending – that is, putting the sounds and letters in words together to make a word. If they have this difficulty, reading can be an ordeal as each word will need to be sounded out and processed, and this can be time-consuming and disheartening. It will also have an impact on the meaning of the story – that is, reading comprehension. This in turn can influence the child's enjoyment of reading.

Memory

Children with dyslexia can have memory difficulties – that can be short-term or working memory, or indeed long-term memory problems. Working memory difficulties can be seen when the child is processing two or more pieces of information at the same time. In the assessment, a backwards number span test is often used for this, as this involves a number of activities such as remembering the numbers, putting them in order and then saying them backwards. They may also have long-term memory difficulties. This means they need a great deal of overlearning and repetition before they can retain information fully.

Processing speed

People with dyslexia often have a weakness or difficulty with processing speed – that is, their pace of work does not match their processing ability. This has the obvious effect that pupils can run out of time in finishing work. It can also mean that comprehension of text is difficult, because material is being processed too slowly for the child to get the 'flow' of the text, and indeed for him or her to get enjoyment out of reading. Slow processing can affect the pupil's ability to produce developed and structured written work.

We often find that pupils with processing speed difficulties have developed the habit of working quickly to keep up, and they will sometimes rush through tasks and complete before the allocated time. Of course, it is more likely than not that this strategy will lead to a higher level of mistakes, which can be very discouraging for the pupil who feels he or she has worked hard to meet requirements.

Co-ordination
There are other factors that can be noted in an assessment, such as motor and co-ordination difficulties, and organisational difficulties that can accompany them. These can be important in gathering evidence for an SpLD, such as dyslexia or perhaps dyspraxia.

It is also quite common for children with dyslexia to have writing difficulties – there could be handwriting difficulties, and/or difficulties in written expression. In written expression, they may know what they want to write, but have difficulty in expressing it in writing.

Discrepancies and variations in scores
Children with dyslexia can often show variations in the results of the individual tests. These are often called discrepancies. Children with dyslexia usually have difficulties in processing speed and/or working memory, and the same can apply to those children with dyspraxia. Children with dyspraxia and dyslexia can both experience difficulties with print, but there will be some differences.

For example, children with dyslexia may have higher scores in some visual areas but lower scores in language aspects – particularly reading and/or decoding of print. Another quite common discrepancy is that between decoding, on the one hand, and reading or listening comprehension, on the other. They may have good skills in comprehension, but their reading difficulties, and particularly their difficulties with decoding, prevent them from displaying these skills. This discrepancy between decoding and comprehension can be quite common. They may also show a variation between reasoning, or understanding and processing skills – memory and speed. These discrepancies can be seen in the cognitive assessment, for example the WISC 5 or WAIS 4, which are shown in Appendix 1.

There can be a discrepancy between oral and written responses – orally the child may be quite competent, and some can be very skilled in this area – but he or she can have a significant difficulty with written expression. Discrepancies can also be noted in class performance, and within the different subject areas of the curriculum.

Differences

It is also important to acknowledge the differences between individual learners. This particularly applies to dyslexic children. An assessment, therefore, should consider learning and cognitive styles, as well as the learning and teaching environment. An appreciation of this can help to effectively link assessment and teaching. This also helps to take the child's preferences for learning into account. This should be a key factor in an assessment. Some of those factors, such as a preference to process information visually, can be seen during the assessment, but information on how the child performs in class with different types of tasks can be important, and the teacher can provide this type of information.

CASE STUDY

Background

Janice is nine years old, and has a difficulty with reading, spelling and writing. She is now beginning to become more aware of her difficulties. This is becoming quite significant, and is causing concern. This has prompted the referral for an assessment. She does have significant difficulties with reading, and this is having an impact across the curriculum.

Results

Cognitive

In the assessment, Janice scored in the high average range, in the 81st percentile in verbal comprehension. This is a very good score, and she has an excellent understanding of language concepts and a good oral vocabulary. Her fluid reasoning, which relates to visual understanding, was also in the high average range, in the 79th percentile. Her visual spatial index score was in the very high range, in the 97th percentile. The visual spatial index relates to skills that can be useful in design, technology and perhaps maths.

Janice's processing speed was in the low average range, and her working memory was also in the low average range. Both were in the 14th percentile.

Janice has the potential to perform to a very high standard, but she does have a significant difficulty with reading, and this will have an impact on her performances across the curriculum.

Attainments

In the WIAT 3 single word reading test, Janice scored in the 8th percentile, and she has difficulties with sight word recognition and also decoding (word attack skills). This means she will have difficulty in reading new words. In the GORT 5 oral reading in context test, she scored in the low average level for accuracy, and her reading comprehension and reading speed were in the below average range.

Janice's practical number work came out in the average range, but in the lower end of average. In the maths problem-solving sub-test, however, she scored comfortably in the average range. Her maths speed was on the low side.

In tests of phonological processing speed, Janice showed a significant delay in her speed of reading numbers and letters.

Phonological awareness

Janice showed difficulties in tests of phonological awareness and in her memory for word sounds (phonemes). She also showed a lack of fluency in reading sight words and non-words. This is likely to make it hard for her to decode, or to spell, unfamiliar words. This in turn could affect her fluency in reading, and her comprehension.

Accommodations and supports
Examination supports

- Janice will need extra time for all reading and writing activities in class and in exams.

- Janice will also need extra time for maths.

- As she progresses with her keyboard skills, it will be better if Janice can use a laptop in future examinations. This should be considered as a longer-term aim.

Classroom support for learning

- Copying notes from the board or book should be minimised, as this will take Janice longer.

- Janice will need a structure for all written work, including front-loaded (pre-taught) vocabulary.

- Janice should eventually be encouraged to compose her own notes and to access strategies such as mind mapping which can be useful for this. (In mind mapping, the child uses a diagram to visually organise information.)

- Janice will need support with structuring and organising written work, and she will need more time to complete written work in class. This can have implications for homework. Homework can take her a long time, and this should be reviewed.

- Janice needs to further develop her reading accuracy and her reading fluency. She should also try to access inferential reading, therefore looking more deeply at the implications of what the author is indicating. We need the skills of inferential reading to understand information in the text that is not stated directly, but has to be inferred from the context.

- It is also a good idea to encourage Janice to become more independent and confident as a learner, and to encourage self-study strategies.

- It is important to consider Janice's self-esteem, as she is aware of her challenges and this can have an impact on the development of her reading and writing skills.

Some points to consider in the above case study

Janice does have literacy issues, particularly with spelling and written work. She also has maths difficulties, but not to the same extent as her reading and writing. Her profile indicates that she has dyslexia, due to her low levels of reading, her difficulties in phonological awareness and her low performances in working memory and processing speed tasks.

Janice will require support with reading, and more time for reading in class. She will need a great deal of support with spelling and writing and also support to develop her general confidence in learning.

Janice's cognitive profile indicates that she will need exam accommodations such as extra time and also additional support in class.

It is important to focus on Janice's strengths, to encourage her to develop her creativity and imagination, and to help to translate these into written work. She will need a lot of support and encouragement for this.

It is important to ensure that Janice's current challenges in processing information and literacy do not detract from the development of her higher-order thinking skills, and she will benefit from activities that focus on her creativity and her strengths. It should be noted that her oral language comprehension is high, so she is capable of understanding books to a high level, if they are read to her. Some of the ideas for inferential reading and critical literacy can also be helpful.

It is crucial that Janice's confidence is developed and her self-esteem considered. It is important that she gains more independence in learning.

Janice's homework needs to be clearly explained to her, so that she understands what has to be done. It is also important to note that homework will take her a long time and this needs to be considered in the setting of work at home. Janice will benefit from consistency in order to make her feel secure in the learning situation.

Overlap

There is a growing body of research that highlights the overlap between a range of SpLDs. SpLD can include dyslexia, dyspraxia, dysgraphia, dyscalculia and some other conditions such as auditory processing difficulties, and elements of attention difficulties. There is therefore a likelihood of two or more learning difficulties co-occurring within the same child. This can make the assessment and diagnosis, and particularly the recommendations, more challenging. For example, a child with dyslexia and an attention deficit may require different teaching interventions compared to a child with dyslexia alone.

There are also some well-researched studies showing overlaps between dyslexia and dyspraxia (co-ordination difficulties). Everatt and Reid (2009) note that some children with dyspraxia also have difficulties with phonological processing and auditory memory, and therefore their profile can also be associated with dyslexic difficulties. Reid and Guise (2017) have mapped the overlaps that exist between a number of SpLDs and the challenges that result from these difficulties, and have noted that factors such as processing speed, literacy attainments, attention, self-esteem, memory, expressive writing and organisation can be challenges in a number of overlapping conditions.

School-based assessment

School assessments can be ongoing, and used to monitor progress as well as to identify difficulties. Usually, the teacher will have an idea if the child is experiencing significant difficulties with any aspect of the curriculum, and the school assessment can be used to confirm this.

If the regular school assessment finds a student with significant difficulties in any area, then it is likely that the teacher will discuss this with the learning support teacher, or school SENCo (Special Educational Needs Co-ordinator), or equivalent. Learning support teachers will usually have some tests at their disposal and can assess accordingly. The school may also have access to a specialist teacher assessor who can also access most attainment and ability tests.

Some of the tests that are likely to be carried out at school are detailed in Appendix 1. It is likely that when school assessments are carried out, there will be an emphasis on basic attainments – that is, reading, spelling, writing and maths. These also usually look for any discrepancies – for example, if there are any significant differences between oral and written responses, and also any differences between various aspects of reading. For example, reading accuracy may be okay, but the child may have a difficulty with reading comprehension. This often happens with children with dyslexia, as they overfocus on reading accuracy and as a result may overlook comprehension. It is also useful to look at reading speed (fluency), as this can impact on reading comprehension. If the child is reading at a slow rate, then he or she may not obtain full comprehension from the text.

Research carried out in Scotland on SpLDs, including dyslexia, indicated that, as a procedure, observation rated very highly (Reid, Deponio and Davidson-Petch 2005). This included systematic teacher observation, as well as more informal observation and 'dynamic assessment' – describing the pupil's strengths and weaknesses and suggesting the type of supports that would be most useful.

Interestingly, over 30 different tests or procedures were used by the education authorities in this study. Many education authorities preferred to operate a staged process of identification which included liaison with support for learning staff, teacher observation at age 4–5, interim screening at ages 5–6 and 6–7, a home visiting service and parental discussion.

Many education authorities would view the identification of dyslexia as an ongoing process of information-gathering over a period of time, rather than from the results of a single test, but would appreciate the importance of a battery of tests and of formal assessments from qualified professionals such as practitioner psychologists and teachers with specialist qualifications in this area. It is important for schools to recognise the accessibility of different tests in terms of the qualifications of staff using these. This is shown in Appendix 1.

The role of parents

It is important for parents to have good communication links with the school. Parents can have a number of anxieties relating to the need for their children to reach their potential, and it is important that these anxieties are discussed with the school. Parents should have a key role throughout the school assessment. This will help to strengthen the communication process between home and school, which has been shown to be of significant importance in measured outcomes of progress in literacy.

What role, therefore, can parents play in an assessment? Parents usually know their child very well and can note, for example, the differences in the learning pattern and skills between different children in the same family. They may note that one child, for example, may take longer to master the alphabet, may be more reluctant to read than others, may be more forgetful, or may be even a bit clumsy or lacking in co-ordination.

Many of these things can be quite normal and merely highlight the normal individual differences between children – even children in the same family. But if parents are concerned, it is usually for a reason, and every professional needs to treat that concern seriously. Parents may be concerned if they know someone with dyslexia, or have read about dyslexia, and see some similarities between these observations and their knowledge of their own child. Communication between home and school is vitally important in both the identification and the support of the young child with dyslexia.

Classroom pointers

What are the pointers of 'high risk' of dyslexia that teachers should look for in the classroom? The important point to make is that it is not *one* factor but a cluster of characteristics that should raise alarm bells. Some of those characteristics can be noted by considering the following.

Attention span

- Is the child distracted easily, particularly when engaged in literacy work?

- Is he or she less distractible when involved in an active, 'hands-on' activity?

- He or she may prefer to be engaged in a practical task.

- Is he or she more engaged when working with others? Often, children with dyslexia prefer to work in groups, or with another person.

Structure

- Is the child able to structure his or her own work, or does he or she need support in this area?

- Does he or she find it difficult to make a start with work?

- Often, once the child gets that initial support, he or she progresses quite well.

- Children with dyslexia often have difficulty in structuring their work, and often need some initial support to get started.

Memory

Does he or she:

- often lose his or her possessions?

- tend to be quite forgetful?

- require a lot of repetition, and have difficulty in retaining information even once learnt?

Sequencing

Does he or she:

- have difficulties following a sequence, for example in a story, or in carrying out instructions in sequence?
- put letters out of sequence in spelling or in written work?

Language

Does he or she:

- manage to express what he or she means orally, or is this difficult?
- manage to describe something clearly, or does he or she have difficulties in conveying the meaning accurately?
- tend to mispronounce words?

Reading

Does he or she:

- have difficulties in reading aloud?
- tend to be a hesitant and reluctant reader?
- have difficulty in discriminating between letters that look alike, or sound alike?
- transpose parts of a word, or letters in a word?
- have difficulties with initial, medial or end sounds?
- have difficulty in blending or decoding a word?
- have difficulty in remembering the letters that make specific sounds?

Comprehension

Does he or she:

- have difficulties with reading comprehension?

- manage to transfer concepts and ideas he or she has come across in reading comprehension to other or previous learning?

- require more explanation than you would expect to give?

Motivation and responsibility

- Can the child show an unusual level of reluctance when it comes to reading, compared to other activities?

- Note when motivation is increased – perhaps this can be through cues and support, or working with others.

- Is he or she reluctant to take responsibility for his or her own learning?

- Note the type of help that is required.

Self-esteem

- Is the child's confidence low?

- Does his or her level of self-concept and overall confidence differ significantly, depending on the task?

- Is the child relaxed when learning, or tense?

Learning preferences

It may also be worthwhile at this point to note if the child has any learning preferences. For example, auditory – prefers to listen; or visual – prefers to see something before he or she can fully understand or process it.

- Does he or she prefer to talk rather than read?

- Is he or she more comfortable working on an activity – for example, using the kinaesthetic and tactile modalities?

- Does he or she prefer to know the 'big picture' when reading – that is, what the story is about and the characters, etc.? Children with dyslexia may have difficulty with the smaller components of the reading process, but can be more comfortable asking questions about the overall story.

Planning

The importance of planning cannot be understated, and students with dyslexia can have significant difficulties with this. This can be particularly frustrating for students. They can have difficulty in identifying key points, particularly in written work. They may also have difficulties with introductions and conclusions, and generally planning an answer to a question. Additional time can help with this, as they can allocate time solely for planning.

The cognitive assessment and information-processing

Information-processing should be a key focus of an assessment, and this is a cognitive activity. Information-processing describes how information is presented (input), how the information is understood, memorised and learnt (cognition), and how it is displayed by the learner (output), and this can be in a written or oral form.

The factors within the information-processing cycle are important in relation to dyslexia, because children with dyslexia often have difficulty in actually receiving the information (input), particularly if it is provided verbally. This can have implications for the use of standardised tests, which are often administered verbally, and where the child has to process the information using the auditory modality.

Children with dyslexia can have difficulties in relation to cognition. Cognition refers to how children think and process information in order to understand it, how they relate the information to previous knowledge, and how it is organised and stored in long-term memory. Since these areas can represent difficulties often associated with dyslexia, there is a tendency to focus on these cognitive factors in a full assessment.

An independent full assessment can provide sufficient information on the cognitive processes involved in learning, and together with information on the attainment pattern can identify the presence of dyslexia.

Independent assessment

It may be necessary to obtain an independent assessment. This is normally carried out by a registered practitioner psychologist, who is able to access tests which are not available to other professionals (see Appendix 1).

This type of assessment – a psycho-educational assessment – involves reviewing background information, conducting the assessment, providing feedback on the test results, preparing a written report with recommendations, and sometimes meeting with families and/or school staff, or other professionals.

Self-advocacy

One of the major challenges facing teachers of pupils with dyslexia is the need to fully appreciate and understand the perspectives and the experiences of the pupil. Ideally, this should be tackled in a positive and meaningful way. It can be suggested that pupils should have more scope for self-advocacy.

It is important that the child has some awareness of dyslexia, what it is, and how it may affect learning, and subject and career choice. Ideally, dyslexia should place no limitations at all on the learner, particularly if the school system is an inclusive one. It is helpful if time is taken to explain to the dyslexic child exactly how he or she can cope with dyslexia, and any difficulties that may arise from this – but also to highlight the strengths. The child may be concerned about any stigma, real or imagined, that may arise from the dyslexia label. There may well be a need to educate staff and the child's peer group about what dyslexia is. Friendship and acceptance by a child's peer group is important.

Summary

As indicated in Chapter 2, there is a wide range of tests and procedures that can be used to identify dyslexia. But the important points are that dyslexia needs to be recognised, and that any results from an assessment are acted on and fully implemented into the child's learning programme. An assessment will provide pointers for intervention; this is an important aspect of any assessment. This is also an area where there are many choices and resources available, and this further underlines the importance of a full and detailed professional assessment, as it will help teachers and parents in their choice of programmes and strategies for the child. This is discussed in the following chapter.

Chapter 5

Assessment and Impact on Learning

We have indicated throughout this book that assessment should link with practice. One of the key components of an assessment report is therefore the recommendations section. This should include practical approaches that can be implemented by the school, as well as suggestions for the parents, and strategies that can be used by the learner. The aim of these recommendations should be to help the child to develop more effective learning skills and, very importantly, independence in the learning process. Helping learners to become independent would mean that they can tackle questions with less external support. This is a learning process, and it can take time – for some learners, a long time – and this needs to be appreciated.

This chapter will discuss some of the components of the assessment that can link to intervention and classroom practice. We will also refer here to the potential difficulties that children with dyslexia can experience at school, and particularly with reading, and the strategies that can support them as they work through the curriculum.

Classroom/curriculum assessment

The points below, although principally aimed at the teacher, are also important for parents. These are points that can be discussed in parent/teacher meetings, and it is therefore important that parents are aware of them.

Although individual tests are an important part of an assessment, it is useful to view the assessment process in terms of overcoming 'barriers to learning' (that is, what is preventing the child from learning successfully) rather than through a child-deficit focus (that is, focusing on what the child cannot do). It is important to identify the barriers to learning in relation to the curriculum, and particularly curriculum objectives.

This means looking at how curriculum objectives are identified, assessing the extent to which the child has met them, and deciding what action may be needed to help the child to meet the objectives more fully. These points can link the assessment with intervention. It may be necessary after the assessment to redefine curriculum objectives or the components of an IEP (Individual Education Plan) or similar (an Individualized Education Program in the USA), to make them more accessible for the learner.

Assessment within the curriculum

The purpose of curriculum-based tests is to enable the teacher or assessor to make judgements about a student's level of performance in the classroom, and about his or her rate of progress. It is important therefore to find out the following:

- What is the child finding challenging?

- How fluent is the child at reading – which books can the child read fluently and which does he or she have difficulty with?

- What is the child's level of understanding of tasks and text?

- What is the child's level of vocabulary, comprehension, written work and spelling?

It is also important to note or receive information on the extent to which the child does the following:

- identifies the letters of the alphabet in upper and lower case

- reads aloud with other children

- chooses to spend time looking at books

- understands the relationship between print and illustrations and the role and purpose of illustrations

- uses a range of strategies to read familiar text

- identifies words that start or end with the same or different sounds

- shows understanding of the structure of text by retelling, or predicting content.

Investigating reading difficulties

Although children with dyslexia can have difficulties in all aspects of literacy – reading, spelling and writing – reading is perhaps the key issue. Dyslexia is essentially a reading difficulty. Although there are associated difficulties that can still be present when reading is no longer the major concern, reading problems are the issues that are readily obvious in young children, and often the issue that results in a formal referral for an assessment.

The type of reading errors/difficulties or reading issues that can be noted in an assessment include:

- **Decoding difficulties** – this refers to a difficulty in recognising word patterns and the sounds these patterns make. For example, in the word 'lace' the second letter makes a long 'a' sound, while in the word 'lack' the 'a' sound is short. Once basic rules have been mastered by the child, then he or she will be able to read other words with similar patterns. For example, when the word 'lace' is learnt, the child will be able to read 'face', 'pace' and 'brace'. Using the word 'lack', the child will be able to read 'back', 'sack' and 'black'. Decoding means being able to pull the letters apart to look for familiar patterns.

- **Reading rules** – this will involve a difficulty with remembering rules in reading, particularly silent letters, for example in words where the letter 'e' at the end is not pronounced – as in 'late' – and also in the example above – 'lace'.

- **Omissions** – the child may omit a word when reading, or might miss out a letter in a word. This can be due to a visual issue with reading, or it might be because the child is reading for meaning (this is discussed below).

- **Substitutions** – this is a very common practice for learners with dyslexia. They often read for meaning, and may substitute (usually) an appropriate word for the word that is on the page. For example, they may read 'car' when in fact the word is 'bus'. They may also make substitutions for words that are visually similar such as 'chase' for 'choose'.

- **Reading fluency difficulties** – children with dyslexia often do learn to read accurately, but what we frequently find is that their reading speed is lagging. This can also have an impact on reading comprehension. When assessing reading, it is often important to look at reading speed and reading comprehension, as well as reading accuracy.

Different subject(s) assessment

Some subjects at school may have very specific barriers that can be challenging for the learner with dyslexia. For example, in Science the student may find following a sequence of instructions is challenging, and in History, his or her difficulties may be related to memory, organisation and problems with categorising information. Examples of this would be difficulties in:

- appreciating the relevance of information or ideas – that is, identifying key points
- arranging a list of historical facts into text, and using this to answer a question
- evaluating the evidence, and what might be the most important
- using an extended vocabulary to express ideas.

In mathematics, the barriers may relate to the following:

- the concepts and ideas may be too abstract
- often, rules play a key role in mathematics, and students with dyslexia can have difficulties in learning and consolidating these rules
- the learner may confuse maths symbols, such as plus and minus signs.

Other mathematical skills that may be difficult for children with dyslexia are:

- the visual/spatial skills that are needed to help understand shape, symmetry, size and quantity
- the linear skills that are needed to help understand sequence, order and the representations found in the number system.

Working memory difficulties and slow speed of processing can also have implications for mathematics.

Metacognitive/dynamic assessment

Metacognitive assessment, sometimes called dynamic assessment, is an example of formative assessment. It will not provide a diagnosis, but can provide information on how the child is learning, and the barriers that are preventing successful learning. This type of assessment focuses on the *process* of learning, and the emphasis is on the strategies being used by the learner. It can also be a useful link to teaching, and can help to show the learner's level of independence and his or her thinking and problem-solving abilities.

An example of this is reciprocal teaching, which consists of a dialogue between teacher and student for the purpose of jointly constructing the meaning of text, and therefore can combine assessment with teaching. Information on reciprocal teaching can be found at:

www.readingrockets.org/strategies/reciprocal_teaching

Reciprocal teaching is an active learning procedure that encourages students to think about how they are learning new pieces of information. It also teaches them to ask the right type of questions to enhance their understanding of a piece of text or a book. Although standardised assessment (tests) can give an indication of the student's level of attainments and provide information to compare the student with others of the same age range, tests are essentially a static form of assessment. They emphasise what the learner can do unaided. They do not focus to any great extent on the learner's thinking processes. Metacognitive/dynamic assessment is, in contrast, adaptable.

This is particularly relevant for children with dyslexia, because quite often they have to be shown how to learn, and the connections between, for example, previous learning and new learning need to be highlighted. Metacognition has an important role in learning, and can help to develop thinking skills and provide an awareness of the learning processes and how strategies are used when learning new material. The teacher has an instrumental role to play in assessing metacognitive awareness and in supporting its development. This can be done by asking the student some fundamental questions, and also through observing the learning behaviour of students, such as that indicated in the example below.

When tackling a new task, does the student demonstrate self-assessment by asking questions such as:

- Have I done this before?

- How did I tackle it?

- What did I find easy?

- What was difficult?

- Why did I find it easy or difficult?

- What did I learn?

- What do I have to do to accomplish this task?

- How should I tackle it?

- Should I tackle it the same way as before?

Developing a learning plan through assessment

It is important that an assessment is used to develop an IEP (Individual Education Plan; or, in the USA, an Individualized Education Program) for that child. Some factors that can inform the development of a learning plan include:

- **Knowledge of the child's strengths and difficulties** – this is essential, particularly since not all children with dyslexia will display the same profile. This is therefore the best starting point, because strengths can often be used to help deal with any weaknesses. For example, dyslexic children often prefer visual and kinaesthetic learning, and may have a difficulty with certain types of auditory learning. Phonics, which rely heavily on sounds, and focus on the auditory modality, need to be introduced together with visual and experiential forms of learning. The tactile modality, involving touch and feeling the shape of letters that make specific sounds, should also be utilised.

- **Current level of literacy acquisition** – an accurate and full assessment of the child's current level of attainments is necessary in order to effectively plan a programme of learning. The assessment can include listening comprehension as well as reading accuracy and fluency. Listening comprehension can often be a useful guide to the abilities and understanding of dyslexic children. The discrepancy between listening comprehension and reading accuracy can be one of the key factors in identifying dyslexia.

- **Cultural factors** – background knowledge, particularly relating to cultural factors, is important because it can influence the selection of books and whether some of the concepts in the text need to be singled out for additional and differentiated explanation (Kormos and Smith 2010; Gray 2016; Guise *et al.* 2016). Cultural values are an important factor.

It has been suggested that the 'big dip' in performance noted in some bilingual children in later primary school in the UK may be explained by a failure of professionals to understand and appreciate the cultural values, and the actual level of competence of the bilingual child, particularly in relation to conceptual development and competence in thinking skills (Landon 2001).

It is possible for teachers to misinterpret bilingual children's development of good phonic skills in the early stages of literacy development in English, and they may in fact fail to note the difficulties that these children might be having with comprehension. When the difficulties later emerge, these children can be grouped inappropriately with native speakers of English who have the more conventional problems with phonic awareness, or their difficulties may be assumed to derive from specific perceptual problems rather than from the cultural unfamiliarity of the text.

Strategies for curriculum access

An assessment report should include strategies for dealing with the difficulties experienced by the learner. These strategies can be individual-type strategies, for example to help improve memory or reading skills, but they can also relate to curriculum access. It is important to find out how the child copes with different elements of the school curriculum. This can refer to different subject areas, or different types of activities within the curriculum.

Below are some strategies that can be used to help the student with dyslexia to overcome the barriers that may prevent curriculum access:

- **Talk** – discussion is crucial for most children with dyslexia, as it is an active and interactive form of learning. This provides them with more involvement in the learning process. Discussion can be used both in learning and assessment, and can help the teacher to monitor the child's progress and understanding of the topic. Although they can be quite comfortable orally, some children with dyslexia can have difficulty in sequencing phrases and in structuring language. When retelling a story, for example, they may get the general gist of the story, but omit some detail. They may also get key pieces of information out of order.

- **Drama** – as indicated above, talk and discussion can be very important for learners with dyslexia. Drama uses the kinaesthetic (experiential) modality, and can also help with memory, and indeed with confidence.

- **Drawing** – visual representation can be a helpful tool for many learners with dyslexia. This would often be noted in an assessment, when, for example, the learner uses visual strategies to remember information. It is a good idea to ask the learner what strategies he or she used for memorising lists of information. Drawing can help with creativity, but it can also help the learner to practise visual representations that can be used in other contexts as a memory aid.

- **Listening** – all learners need to develop listening skills. For some, this can be challenging. It is important that listening is given a high priority, and this is extremely crucial for children with dyslexia, particularly if they are apt to be distracted. Discussion is a good medium for developing listening skills.

- **Role-play** – this can be an excellent tool for developing imagination. It helps to facilitate children's creativity and furthermore can make learning individual. This is very important for children with dyslexia. Additionally, role-play uses the kinaesthetic modality, and this experiential type of learning can benefit children with dyslexia.

Differentiation and assessment

Differentiation refers to teaching that takes account of the difference between where a learner is now, and where he or she has the potential to be. It is not only about making the task and the texts more accessible for students with dyslexia, but also about making the assessment more appropriate and useful. This means using more than one means of noting a child's achievements. Often, children with dyslexia do not perform to their best in standard types of assessment, so other ways of testing their knowledge and understanding can be used. These could include drama, role-play, oral presentations, group work and portfolio work.

It is important to have an assessment process that is able to accommodate the diversity of learners, and not only those who learn a certain way. Both teaching and assessment should be differentiated and diversified. This can be achieved by using a range of assessment procedures focusing on a range of different types of tasks. These can include formal speech-making, journal-keeping, creative writing, poetry, verbal debate and storytelling as a means of assessing some aspects of language abilities. This can also strengthen the link between assessment and teaching.

Subject barriers

As has been mentioned, it is important for parents to be aware of the subject barriers that their child can experience. Mathematics is one example of this.

Mathematics

Abstract concepts and ideas can be difficult for students with dyslexia, as these concepts require organisation and access to knowledge, rules, techniques, skills and concepts. Often, rules that play an important part in mathematics have to be rote-learned. This can prove demanding for dyslexic students, and in addition they still have the literacy and other difficulties associated with dyslexia, such as working memory, speed of processing and automaticity. These can all have implications for mathematics. They may understand the meaning of words such as 'difference', 'evaluate', 'odd', 'mean' and 'product', but then find that they have a quite different meaning in the context of mathematics. They may also confuse small words such as 'for' and 'of', meaning that they do the wrong thing entirely.

The following factors can also contribute to the demands of mathematics for students with dyslexia:

- **Linear and sequential processing** – this can be demanding, because dyslexic students usually have some difficulty with order and sequencing, and yet in some mathematical problems logic and sequence are crucial in order to obtain the correct response.

- **Working memory** – this can also present some difficulties because it is used to hold information in the short-term store, which could be only a few seconds, and process that information into meaningful stimuli. This is very important in mathematics as mental operations are necessary, and this can be demanding for students with dyslexia.

- **Long-term memory and information retrieval** – these can be problematic for students with dyslexia. Much of this is due to the lack of organisation at the cognitive level – that is, at the initial stage of learning. If learning is not organised at this crucial initial stage, then retrieval will be difficult at a later stage.

Useful resources (links and apps for maths learning difficulties and dyscalculia)

10 maths apps: www.parents.com/kids/education/math-and-science/10-playful-math-activities

Information on maths tutoring: http://scopeblog.stanford.edu/2015/09/09/one-on-one-tutoring-relieves-math-anxiety-in-children-stanford-study-finds; https://www.understood.org/en/school-learning/tutors/types-of-tutoring/tutoring-kids-with-dyscalculia-what-you-need-to-know

Maths anxiety: http://scopeblog.stanford.edu/2015/09/09/one-on-one-tutoring-relieves-math-anxiety-in-children-stanford-study-finds

Maths game: https://itunes.apple.com/us/app/power-of-2/id820639638?mt=8

Maths symbols and terms: https://itunes.apple.com/us/app/math-symbols-and-terms/id800894138?mt=8

Maths video guide: www.bbc.co.uk/skillswise/maths

Maths vocabulary cards: https://itunes.apple.com/us/app/math-vocabulary-cards-by-the-math-learning-center/id828601911?mt=8

Communication, Access, Literacy and Learning (CALL) Scotland

Call Scotland have produced a very useful wheel of iPad apps for dyscalculia/numeracy difficulties:

www.callscotland.org.uk/downloads/posters-and-leaflets/ipad-apps-for-learners-with-dyscalculianumeracy-difficulties

Call Scotland also provide a wheel of android apps for dyslexic learners and those with reading or writing difficulties:

www.callscotland.org.uk/downloads/posters-and-leaflets/android-apps-for-learners-with-dyslexia

Other difficulties

Dyspraxia

Dyspraxia is a difficulty with co-ordination and movement, and as has already been indicated, it can overlap with dyslexia. Some of the recommendations and supports for dyspraxia can therefore be similar to those for dyslexia, but some additional and specific pointers are shown below.

Support for dyspraxia can include the following:

- developing and improving organisational skills in a range of different activities

- planning the school week or providing a day-to-day approach by structuring the activities that have to be carried out

- time management to encourage the child to use time efficiently

- thinking through, planning, organising and drafting written work

- reading comprehension techniques (see, for example, the information on reciprocal teaching in relation to dyslexia given earlier in this chapter)

- organising and managing oral information for class presentations

- organising notes, notebook and folders

- reducing stress – for example, by using relaxation exercises.

Dysgraphia

While dyspraxia encompasses organisation and both gross and fine motor skills, dysgraphia focuses on fine motor skills and particularly handwriting.

Support for dysgraphia can include the following:

- Consider using alternatives to handwritten responses, such as a laptop or iPad (a full-sized keyboard is recommended).

- Ensure that the child is not being penalised for poor presentation of work, or misspellings.

- Provide guidelines for structuring written work, such as introduction, paragraph headings and conclusion.

- Mind mapping and bullet points can help with planning and organising written work.

- Ensure that the most up-to-date software is available, and that the spellchecker is appropriate for a child with dyslexia.

- The child with dysgraphia will need rest periods when extended handwriting is required.

Auditory processing difficulties

These are also often referred to as Central Auditory Processing Difficulties (CAPD).

Close monitoring of the child with CAPD is very important to ensure that he or she has understood the instructions for carrying out a task. It is also important to hold his or her attention prior to a task and, very importantly, to keep the task short so that he or she can complete it.

The following website provides a good overview and recommendations for auditory processing difficulties:

www.understood.org/en/school-learning/partnering-with-childs-school/instructional-strategies/classroom-accommodations-for-auditory-processing-disorder

Some other suggestions for support include:

- Avoid too much environmental distraction.

- Keep instructions to a minimum – and deliver them one at a time if possible.

- Provide reassurance on tasks.

- Split tasks into shorter stages, with frequent breaks.

- 'Scaffold' the work to support the child and to help with comprehension – this could include providing cues and helping the child to make connections.

- Try to use visual cues and modelling before a task, so that the child has a good idea of what is involved.

Impact of an assessment

It is important at the outset to ascertain how the assessment can aid intervention. Every attempt should be made to link the information obtained from the assessment to a teaching programme or to aspects of the child's curriculum.

The assessment should also uncover some explanations for the child's difficulties, and look for particular patterns, such as errors that may be due to visual, auditory, motor, memory or some other cognitive difficulties. These may be identified as a specific pattern. The unearthing of a pattern of difficulties can help the assessor and the teacher to decide on the nature of the child's difficulty, and how the information can assist in the planning of an appropriate programme of work.

Strategies for parents

Parents are usually very keen to help their child at home. It is important, however, that the approaches used are consistent with the school and that good communication between home and school is paramount. Shared reading is often used by parents. It involves the parent reading a sentence, and then the child reading a sentence. The parent can ask questions of the child and vice versa to monitor comprehension.

Some other suggestions for parents that can be used as a follow-up from the assessment are shown below.

Pre-reading discussion

It is important that both parents and teachers engage in pre-reading discussion with children before they start reading the text. There is a body of research that suggests that pre-reading discussion is one of the best predictors of a successful outcome in a reading activity. The following questions, indicating the information we need to think about, can provide a framework for pre-reading discussion:

- Where does the story take place?
- What is the time period?
- Who are the main characters?
- Is there anything unusual about the main characters?

- How does the story start?

- What should we look out for in the story?

- How does the book/story relate to the learner's previous knowledge/experience?

It might be more effective if the parent reads the passage first to the child, or perhaps uses paired reading, where the parent and child read to each other.

Monitoring comprehension

It is also a good idea to monitor comprehension, and to ensure the reader has understood the key points of the book or story. This could be carried out at regular intervals, and for some children it will be necessary to do this at short intervals, such as after every paragraph, page or part of a chapter, depending on the child's level of reading. It is important that parents are aware of this; otherwise the child may spend quite a bit of time and effort reading but get very little from the book.

Many children are so busy decoding and reading for accuracy that they do not realise that they are not comprehending. They might not have the insights to monitor their own comprehension. Parents can help by reading with their child, and stopping regularly to check and make sure the child still comprehends. Then they can encourage the child to use the same strategies when they are reading alone, so that eventually the child learns to monitor his or her comprehension independently.

Reciprocal teaching

Reciprocal teaching aims to help the learner to develop comprehension. The parents can do the reading, or the child and parent can read together, but the important stage is the comprehension of print. After the reading is complete – this can be after each paragraph or chapter, or the whole book – the parent asks the child to summarise what has been read. If anything is not clear, the parent can clarify this, for example by explaining any unfamiliar vocabulary. The learner has to ask some questions about what he or she has read. If the child was being read to, the parent can help with these questions. These might include things such as 'Why do you think this happened?', 'Where did the story take place?', etc. Finally the child has to make predictions about what should happen next. This can also give children a purpose to continue reading, to see if their prediction is correct.

The key points of reciprocal reading or learning are therefore: summarise, clarify, question and predict.

The following websites provide useful information for parents to use when they are concerned about comprehension:

www.bbcactive.com/BBCActiveIdeasandResources/Reciprocal TeachingPromoteInteractiveLearning.aspx

www.readingrockets.org/strategies/reciprocal_teaching

Ideally, children will become independent with this approach, and will eventually learn to monitor their comprehension. Until they are able to do that, however, it is important to put strategies in place that will get them to the point where they will automatically recognise that they do not comprehend, and will know what to do about it. Reciprocal teaching forces them to recognise whether or not they understand what they are reading.

Summary

It is important to acknowledge the range of procedures that can be used in an assessment. It does not always have to rely exclusively on tests, but clearly tests should be a key component if one of the purposes of the assessment is to identify dyslexia. Tests can provide the information needed for a diagnosis, but the information from the assessment can be extended if a wider range of sources is used. School and curriculum assessment have important roles to play. Independent assessments also have a key role to play, as often they can provide data that the school will find useful, but may not be able to provide themselves. The key point is that communication between home and school should be prioritised, and an assessment where each plays a role in providing information and sharing the results is extremely helpful.

Above all, it is important that the assessment should link with practice, and suggestions for intervention are a key part of the assessment. We have discussed this aspect in this chapter, but it is also important that recommendations should be contextualised and individualised for the child with dyslexia.

Chapter 6

Strategies and Resources

This chapter focuses on strategies and resources. Resources have already been suggested throughout the book and in resources sections in some of the chapters, but more are given here to relate to specific strategies. Also, important information will be provided to explain the strategies suggested.

As stated at the start of the book, dyslexia can be described as a learning *difference*. This is because, as noted in earlier chapters, dyslexic learners often have a different cognitive profile. Most commonly, the scores for reasoning ability (verbal and/or visual processing) are higher than the processing scores (working memory and/or speed). That is, the child's processing capacity is not quite keeping up with his or her ability. This can go some way to explaining why it is that the child is experiencing a learning *difficulty* – for example in literacy, or numeracy – and why it is that the child's attainments do not seem to match his or her potential.

It follows, then, that we should take a multi-faceted approach to helping the dyslexic child.

This will involve:

- consolidating the core literacy skills
- providing support to compensate for weaker cognitive processing
- working to improve cognitive processing skills
- maintaining/improving self-esteem and confidence.

These four areas will be discussed below. More generally, we need to be aware of the following key principles that should form the basis of all support:

- **Collaboration** – it is very important for parents to work in collaboration with the school, so that all parties are working in the same direction to properly support the pupil.

- **Overlearning** – the dyslexic pupil will often need to review and revise information more often before it becomes automatic.

- **Multi-sensory teaching and learning** – this is sometimes referred to as 'multi-kinaesthetic' learning. The dyslexic pupil is far more likely to be able to remember information that has been presented in different modalities (not just in print). Incidentally, this type of learning is likely to suit most pupils, because of the variety and the practical, hands-on approaches used. It is also more interesting, and satisfying, for teachers and parents to use multi-sensory methods, particularly given the need for overlearning noted above. A range of tried and tested activities can be found in Reid, Guise and Guise (2018).

- **'Knowing how we know'** – this is also called 'metacognition'. It is extremely helpful for all pupils, but particularly those who are dyslexic, to have an understanding of how they learn best.

- **Independent learning** – the ultimate aim of support and strategies is for the pupil to become an independent learner, who can transfer skills and strategies to new situations in other contexts, and in future learning.

Consolidating core literacy skills
Phonological processing

A number of structured, systematic phonics programmes are available. They can be used to strengthen the connections between the basic sounds of English, and how they are written. Many are designed for teachers or trained professionals. The following programmes are aimed at parents, and do not need any specialist background:

- 'Toe by Toe' (for children and adults): www.toe-by-toe.co.uk

- 'Teach Your Child to Read in 100 Easy Lessons': www.startreading.com

- 'Beat Dyslexia' – a series of six books with photocopiable activities, reading and spelling cards and an audio CD. Available from Amazon and other retailers or at: www.ldalearning.com/product/cognition-and-learning/dyslexia-and-literacy/beat-dyslexia/beat-dyslexia-book-1/admt10157

- 'ABC Reading Eggs' (for children aged 2 to 13): https://reading eggs.co.uk/about

- Programmes such as 'Wordshark' can be useful for school and home use. Wordshark combines computer games with procedures for reading and spelling: www.wordshark.co.uk/index.aspx

- The Nessy Programme has many resources, and some can be useful for parents to use at home: www.nessy.com

- Similarly, Jolly Phonics is very useful for young children: www.jollylearning.co.uk/jolly-phonics

- As mentioned above, Call Scotland have produced a very useful wheel of iPad apps for dyscalculia/numeracy difficulties: www.callscotland.org.uk/downloads/posters-and-leaflets/ipad-apps-for-learners-with-dyscalculianumeracy-difficulties

- Call Scotland also provide a wheel of android apps for dyslexic learners and those with reading or writing difficulties: www.callscotland.org.uk/downloads/posters-and-leaflets/android-apps-for-learners-with-dyslexia

The components of reading

The components of reading are explained below. We have used spelling as an example of the strategies that can be used. For strategies on the other components, see *Teach Your Child to Read in 100 Easy Lessons* (Engelmann, Haddox and Bruner 1983).

Phonology and phonological awareness

Phonology is the study of sounds, and a phoneme is the smallest unit of sound. Phonological awareness is the understanding of the internal linguistic structure of words. An important aspect of phonological awareness is **phonemic awareness**, or the ability to segment words into their component sounds.

Sound–symbol association

Sound–symbol association – that is, knowledge of the letters and combinations of letters that represent different sounds – is important for fluent reading. Sound–symbol association can be taught through relating the visual to the auditory stimuli, or vice versa. Young children also need to master the blending of sounds and letters into words, as well as the segmenting of whole words into the individual sounds.

Syllable instruction

A syllable is a unit of oral or written language containing one vowel sound. Instruction must include the teaching of the six basic types of syllables in the English language. These are:

- **Closed** – the most common type. Here, the vowel is short, and the syllable is closed off with one or more consonants; for example, '*bat*-ter'.

- **Vowel-Consonant-e (VCe)** – sometimes referred to as 'magic "e"'. This would have a long vowel spelt with a single letter, then a consonant, then a silent 'e'; for example, '*make*'.

- **Open** – that is, ending with a long vowel sound, with no consonant to close it; for example, '*mo*-ther'.

- **Consonant-le (C-le)** – found only at the end of a word, so it is known as the 'stable final syllable'; for example, 'pud-*dle*'.

- **R-controlled** – sometimes referred to as 'vowel-r' because this is a vowel followed by an 'r'; for example, 'fa-*ther*'.

- **Diphthong**, or 'vowel team' – this can be two, three or four letters and often appears in sight words; for example, '*though*'.

Syllable division rules must be directly taught in relation to the word structure.

Morphology

Morphology is the study of how morphemes are combined from words. A morpheme is the smallest unit of meaning in the language.

Syntax

Syntax is the set of principles that dictate the sequence and function of words in a sentence needed to convey meaning. This includes grammar, sentence variation and the mechanics of language.

Semantics

Semantics is that aspect of language concerned with meaning. The teaching of reading should include, from the beginning, instruction in the comprehension of written language.

Spelling

Broadly, there are two aspects of spelling that have to be addressed.

First, in order to learn regular words, the learner has to develop phonological awareness and fluency. This involves matching sounds with the way that we generally write these sounds in English, and this is discussed above. It is also important to memorise spelling rules.

Second, in English we have a fairly large proportion of words that are not regular. These 'sight' words have to be learnt individually, and in order to do that, the learner has to draw, to a large extent, on visual processing skills and visual memory.

Strategies to help with spelling

The following strategies can be drawn on as appropriate to help with spelling.

Look at words within words. This helps with prefix and suffix combinations. It can also help when reading words with more than one syllable. Using visual cues brings in an additional sense. Another way of increasing the memory trace is to use a magnetic board, and letters that can be moved around. This is also quicker, and can be more enjoyable, than writing and rewriting different versions of a word.

The School Zone has a range of fun activities in spelling:

www.schoolzone.com

Spelling rules will need to be taught explicitly, with overlearning to practise using the rules. Exceptions to spelling rules should only be introduced after a rule has been mastered.

An established strategy for spelling is 'look, cover, write, check':

- **'Look'** involves active engagement of the pupil, who should look closely at the word, with the intention of reproducing it. At this stage, tracing can be used, which uses the tactile sense and motor movement. It is important to spend time looking at the visual features of the word.

- **'Cover'** brings the visual memory into play. Some dyslexic learners have a good visual memory, and they might discover that this strength is useful here. This stage can be turned into a game – ask the child which visual features he or she remembers.

- **'Write'** is an important stage, because it provides the kinaesthetic practice needed to strengthen the memory trace. It should be noted that this method may not be suitable for those children with dysgraphia (a significant handwriting difficulty), or even for some children who have mild difficulties with handwriting. At the same time, it can provide the child with handwriting practice. To make it easier, an adult could write the word and the child could either trace the word, or skip this step.

- **'Check'** provides the learner with some responsibility for his or her own spelling. Research suggests that self-checking is one of the best ways of learning and revising information.

Another technique that can be used is 'simultaneous oral spelling'. The steps for this include the following:

- Have the word written correctly, or made with letters.

- Say the word.

- Write the word, saying each letter as it is written.

- Check to see if the word is correct.

- Cover up the word, and repeat the process.

- Continue to practise the word in this way, three times a day, for a week.

By this time, the word should be committed to memory. However, only one word will have been learnt. The final step involves categorising the word with other words that sound and look alike. So, for example, if the word that has been learnt is 'round', the learner is then shown that he or she can also spell 'ground', 'pound', 'found', 'mound', 'sound', 'around', 'bound', 'grounded', 'pounding', etc. Therefore, a larger number of words have been learned, having put concentrated effort into the 'root' word.

It can be helpful to construct a word list that focuses on the pupil's curriculum.

A computer spellchecker can be useful to help to reinforce correct spelling. While some parents have expressed concerns that this might be detrimental to learning, it can be argued that the spellchecker is a great benefit because it quickly corrects mistakes and quickly reinforces the right spelling. On the plus side, the spellchecker can relieve the pressure of ensuring that spelling is correct, which often detracts from a focus on the content and meaning of the written piece. If children are overfocusing on this, it can restrict their writing to words they can spell. This means that their written work will not do them justice and will not show their real creative abilities and imagination.

Practice in use of homophones

Homophones are words that have the same sound but different meanings and different spellings. The English language has many homophones. Here are some examples:

- there/they're/their
- to/too/two
- been/bean
- bye/buy/by
- here/hear
- pear/pair/pare
- isle/aisle/I'll
- allowed/aloud
- ate/eight
- new/knew
- piece/peace
- genes/jeans.

Homophones can be learned through practice and use. Some over-learning is required until they become automatic.

Strategies to help with reading

As with spelling, at word level we need to look at phonic rules (so that we can decode new or unfamiliar words), and at irregular words, which have to be learnt by sight. The spelling activities above will also help with reading. The next level, after deciphering single words, is comprehension of text. Some dyslexic children find text easier to read than single words, because they become skilled at using the context to guide their reading. However, they can have difficulties when the vocabulary becomes harder, or when texts are longer. Comprehension can be tricky when word reading is slow or hesitant. Often, dyslexic pupils will need to take time to read a text more than once to be able to fully understand it. A number of strategies can help here:

- **Underline or highlight key words**, especially in test or exam questions.

- Use **paired reading** to improve fluency; the pupil can work first with a more able reader, and then might like to work with a younger child who has reading difficulties – this can help build self-esteem.

- Listen to **audio books** while looking at the written version of the book.

- Use **high-interest** materials.

When the child's reading skills have improved, it will be important to develop higher-order thinking skills. This can be done by asking questions about the text at frequent intervals (before, during and after reading). For example:

- What does the title suggest to you?

- Are you enjoying the story? Why?/Why not?

- Who are the main characters? How do you know that?

- What do you think will happen next?

Some questions that can help with consolidating comprehension and concepts after reading are shown below.

- What did you enjoy about the book?

- Was there anything you found confusing about the book?

- Was the plot easy to follow? Why?/Why not?

- What do you think the author was trying to tell the reader?

- Did you like the way the author described the setting?

- What could have been done to create a better picture for you?

- Was this believable? Has the information in the text been distorted, or oversimplified?

It is also important to try to encourage the learner to become more independent, and self-questioning is one way of doing that. Some self-questions for comprehension might include:

- What have I got to do here?

- Do I understand the task?

- What is my plan for completing this reading/task?

- What do I already know about this topic?

- How am I doing?

- Do I need any more information?

- Can I summarise what I have read, in my own words?

These questions will aid comprehension of the task, and allow students to take more control over their own learning.

Written expression

First of all, it is crucial that the child's spelling does not restrict the development of his or her expressive writing. Dyslexic pupils can show great creativity in their ideas, and we do not want in any way to stifle that spark. They can have difficulties with more structured writing, and sometimes need guidance in getting started, and staying on track. The following can be helpful:

- provide a list of **high-frequency words** for reference

- provide a list of **key words**, appropriate to the topic or curriculum

- practise **sentence expansion** – take a selection of vocabulary from a familiar book, make up some phrases using this vocabulary, and then ask the pupil to put these phrases into new sentences

- provide an **opening sentence**, or paragraph.

For extended writing, it is often helpful for the pupil to use a computer. This can make it easier to structure and edit written work.

When the pupil is at an appropriate stage, he or she might find it helpful to use mind maps to plan and structure written work. These can be done manually, or by using a range of computer software programs. We are of the opinion that computers and spellcheckers should be used as early as possible. We say this because if the child habitually misspells a word, the wrong spelling can become ingrained and it will be difficult for the child to unlearn. It is therefore better if the child uses the correct spelling before this habitual use of a misspelling of a word takes over.

Similarly, a computer should be introduced as early as possible for writing, so the child can become familiar with using the computer for written work and become familiar with the conventional structure of writing, such as opening paragraph, main part and conclusion, and the use of punctuation.

Numeracy

Dyslexia can overlap with dyscalculia – where the child has significant difficulties understanding basic maths concepts such as number bonds. However, dyslexia in itself can have an impact on maths, and can hinder the pupil's progress in this subject and in related areas. There are a few reasons for this. The vocabulary of maths can be difficult to understand, and to remember. There can be a tendency to misread operators (for instance, carrying out an addition when it should have been a subtraction), and to transpose numbers when copying them. The following strategies can be helpful:

- **highlight** key words

- systematically **mark up maths symbols** (for example, circle every decimal point, highlight every plus sign in blue, etc.)

- create a **list of steps** involved in carrying out particular types of computation

- use **manipulatives** (practical, hands-on methods) to improve the memory trace

- try using **squared paper** to help with alignment of figures (although some children might find that the extra visual stimulus of a page of squared paper can be hard to process; if so, try paper with larger squares)

- draw a **margin** down the left side to keep the question number separate from the calculation.

The following are useful maths apps and tools:

- **BBC Skillwise** – has a selection of video guides and tasks to help build confidence:

    www.bbc.co.uk/skillswise/maths

- **ModMath** – this program helps people with dysgraphia to understand the mathematical problems, and because of the visual aspects it is likely to benefit dyslexic and dyscalculic students:

    www.modmath.com

- **Math Vocabulary Cards** – these can help students to deepen their conceptual understanding of key terms:

    www.mathlearningcenter.org/resources/apps/math-vocabulary-cards

- **Power of 2!** – this number-match game (available from Amazon and other retailers) can keep the brain active and improve automaticity.

- **Maths symbols and terms on posters** (can be found online) – this helps the student to quickly learn the numerous maths symbols found across several maths areas.

- **Math games** can provide fun and stimulating strategies for different types of activities:

    www.funmaths.com

- *Making Maths Visual and Tactile* by Judy Hornigold is an excellent compendium of games and activities to teach key number skills:

    http://senbooks.co.uk/view-product/Making-Maths-Visual-and-Tactile

    Topics covered include:

    - using counters and cubes

    - dice and dot pattern games

- five and ten frames (rectangular boxes into which counters are placed)

- playing with playing cards

- base ten materials (three-dimensional blocks that can be used to illustrate basic mathematical concepts)

- using Cuisenaire rods (rods that can be used as mathematical learning aids), Numicon (shapes that can be used as a multi-sensory approach to maths), pattern blocks and virtual manipulatives.

Handwriting

Some dyslexic children have difficulties with the clarity and/or the speed of their handwriting, and this can have an important impact on the ability to take notes, and to produce extended writing. Even when handwriting is good, it can be difficult for the dyslexic child to get his or her thoughts down on paper before they are forgotten, and for this reason it is a good idea to consider alternative strategies:

- use **bullet point notes/answers**; these can be developed more fully later, if necessary

- use a **highlighter** to mark where text should be written, if the child has difficulty writing on the line

- encourage the child to **score out once** (and not rub out, write over or obliterate what he or she has written), and to see mistakes as part of the process of handwriting.

In some circumstances – for example, in assessments, or in extended writing – it might be preferable to develop other ways of recording information:

- use **voice recognition** (on android and iPhone apps, or in computer software programs) to record verbal notes

- act as **scribe** – being careful to record his or her ideas so that he or she can take full ownership of what is written

- encourage the child to improve his or her **keyboard skills** – a number of touch-typing programmes are available:

  - BBC DanceMat is free, and is aimed at children aged 7–11

    www.bbc.co.uk/guides/z3c6tfr

- Doorway Online has free activities for single-handed and two-handed typing

    http://doorwayonline.org.uk/activities/typing

- Nessy Fingers is for children aged eight and over

    www.nessy.com/uk/product/nessy-fingers

- English Type is described as 'special needs friendly'

    www.englishtype.com

- Touch Type, Read and Spell is a multi-sensory course that also teaches reading and spelling at the same time. There are UK and USA versions:

    www.ttrs.co.uk/ttrsonline

    www.readandspell.com/us

Supporting cognitive processing skills
Adjustments for working memory difficulties
Extra time
It is important to note here that many of the strategies that will help the child with working memory difficulties will make the task more time-consuming. So, even if the child has a good speed of processing, extra time will often be needed to carry out tasks to the best of his or her ability.

Giving instructions
In general, it is a good idea to break things down into manageable steps. It is likely, for example, that the child will be able to carry out instructions better if they are given one at a time, or if he or she has a written checklist to refer to. For younger children, organisational cards can be used as visual reminders. They can be written, or they can use photographs and symbols, and they can be laminated. As each part of a sequence is completed, the child can remove it from the top of the pile, and refer to the next card.

Attention
There are some adjustments that can help the child to maintain focus if necessary. Some children find it very useful to have something to fidget with (for instance, 'therapeutic putty'), or to have a swivelling

seat cushion that allows for 'dynamic sitting'. While it may suit some, many dyslexic children will find it difficult to concentrate while sitting still in a quiet room. They might prefer to walk up and down, speak their thoughts aloud, write them down on a wallchart, and generally be more active when studying. Although this can seem counter-intuitive to some parents, moving from one thing to another can be the best way for some children to stay focused!

Organisation

When there is a weakness in working memory, it can be difficult to retain information long enough to properly organise it, and the child can have a tendency to forget details, to go off on a tangent because an idea had to be written down before it was forgotten, and then to lose his or her train of thought. This does not only happen with written work. There are strategies we can use that will remove some of the burden on working memory. It is usually more effective if the child has a role in creating the following:

- use **checklists or flowcharts** to guide the child through a task

- develop **habits**, such as always leaving the school bag/keys/shoes in the same place

- use **colour-coding** – for example, Maths in a red folder, English in a blue folder – so that the child can instantly see whether he or she has the right materials to hand.

Adjustments for processing speed difficulties

The obvious adjustment for a processing speed difficulty is to make sure that the child is given enough time to complete a task to his or her ability. It is equally important that the child knows why it is that he or she needs more time. Often, it is best used to organise what he or she was going to write, or do (rather than to write more content).

We often come across children who have a good processing speed, and have to be encouraged to slow down to improve their accuracy. This can be quite hard for the child who has a natural inclination to go fast. Sometimes, when extra time is given, more prompting will be needed to help to keep the child on track.

Improving cognitive processing skills

Improving working memory skills

Retaining instructions

If instructions are kept simple, and consistent, they will be more easily remembered. If the child has some input into the steps, this will also make them more memorable for him or her. He or she could develop a mind map, or other visual reminder, or an audio recording of the steps involved.

Maintaining attention

We find that people often do not realise that the child who is easily distracted is often putting a lot of effort and energy into trying to stay focused. It is very important to acknowledge how tiring, and demoralising, this can be at times. It can also be useful for the child, and the parents, to know that it will not always be possible to stay fully focused. This means that there is likely to be some inconsistency in performance, and that 'silly' mistakes can happen. This is to be expected, and knowing this can help to reduce some of the frustration and annoyance that can be felt by the child, and the parents.

Organisation

Organisational skills can be improved with practice. The child who has learnt to use the techniques and strategies described earlier in this chapter will, in time, be able to apply the principles to other situations. This is far more likely to happen if the strategies are discussed with the child, and if he or she has input into this process.

Improving processing speed

Developing automaticity

The dyslexic child can take longer to develop automaticity, and this is likely to involve a good deal of overlearning, and the use of multi-sensory techniques. It is important to persevere in developing automaticity in core skills, because this will improve fluency. This in turn will improve comprehension in reading, and the level of written expression. Even better – when a skill is automatic, working memory is no longer involved.

Maintaining/improving self-esteem and confidence

Focusing on strengths

It is particularly important to focus on the strengths of the dyslexic child, who often already has a good idea of what he or she cannot do, or finds much harder. Not all children appreciate the skills and talents that they have, or they might undervalue them because they do not always match well to what is measured in class.

When we are giving feedback after an assessment, we often find that we are talking about the same strengths that the parents have already pointed out to the child – but it can make a great difference for the child to hear this from an outsider! It can also help to validate the parent who might be hesitant to seem 'pushy' in their dealings with the school. From the school's point of view, it can be really helpful to know where the stronger areas are, because these will form the basis of the assessment recommendations. Also, knowing that there are strengths provides a good incentive to provide support and accommodations – it is clear that they are likely to improve outcomes for that child.

Self-esteem

When pupils have to work harder to get to the same level, or when they are not able to achieve the same results as their peers, this can lead to difficulties with confidence, and self-esteem. One of the tricky aspects of the dyslexic profile is that the child might have some sense that he or she is just as smart as his or her peers. Yet, things like spelling, reading, writing and numeracy can be much harder, or performance can be much more inconsistent. So, the child then begins to doubt him or herself, and often we are told by parents that the child thinks he or she is stupid. It is very important to try to deal with these conflicting feelings by explaining to the child that dyslexia is a processing difference, and that this means that he or she might find some things take longer to learn, but this is not related to how smart he or she is.

Often, it can be inspiring to think about dyslexic people who have achieved a lot in their lives. Sometimes the parents themselves are good role models here, and there are certainly a number of celebrities from areas such as sport, media, the arts and business who are known to be dyslexic.

Another way to build self-esteem is to gain experience of success in the areas that are difficult. This can be done by making sure that tasks are manageable, and this sometimes means breaking them down into a number of steps that make the larger task easier to tackle.

Resilience

It is important to recognise and acknowledge that being dyslexic can mean that the child will always find some tasks a little harder, or that some types of task might always take a little longer, and that it might at times feel a bit like he or she is moving 'two steps forward, one step back'. It is very important that the child has a realistic idea of the possible difficulties, and the strengths that he or she has to get round them. It is also crucial that the child understands that support and accommodations are simply there to create a level playing field, to make the process of teaching and assessment fairer.

Communication

We have stressed the importance of good communication with the child so that he or she has a sound understanding of why some things might be harder and what can be done by him or her, or by others, to help. It is of course vitally important that parents and teachers also maintain good levels of communication so that everyone is pulling in the same direction to help that child reach his or her potential.

Advocacy

Ultimately, pupils will need to be able to advocate for themselves when they are in different teaching, learning and work environments. For this, they will need the skill of knowing how they learn (metacognition), what their particular strengths and weaknesses are, and what can reasonably be done to help them to achieve their potential. This skill is more likely to emerge if the areas of self-esteem, resilience and communication are properly addressed.

More useful resources
Apps and websites

A list of android apps for dyslexic learners and those with reading or writing difficulties: www.callscotland.org.uk/downloads/posters-and-leaflets/android-apps-for-learners-with-dyslexia

A list of iPad apps for learners with dyslexia: www.callscotland.org.uk/downloads/posters-and-leaflets/ipad-apps-for-learners-with-dyslexia

Dictionary for dyslexic children: https://itunes.apple.com/ca/app/dds-dictionary-a-dyslexics-dictionary/id590239077?mt=8

Dyslexia Quest: https://itunes.apple.com/ca/app/dyslexia-quest/id448166369?mt=8

Phonics with Phonograms: https://itunes.apple.com/ca/app/phonics-with-phonograms-by-logic-of- english/id604337610?mt=8

Read2Me: https://read2me.soft112.com

Sound Literacy: https://itunes.apple.com/ca/app/sound-literacy/id409347075?mt=8

Suggestions of ICT to support learners with dyslexia: www.callscotland.org.uk/common-assets/cm-files/posters/ict-to-support-learners-with-dyslexia.pdf

Rhyming activities

https://fun-a-day.com/even-more-rhyming-activities-for-kids
https://resource-bank.scholastic.co.uk/content/551
https://thelettersofliteracy.com/fun-rhyming-activities-for-kids
https://thisreadingmama.com/printable-rhyming-activities

Spark-Space – enabling software

Spark-Space produce a range of tools to support dyslexics in school, university and the workplace. Its principal products are based on visual thinking and learning and help remove the barriers to producing good quality written work in the shortest possible time. Available at:

www.spark-space.com

Livescribe pen

Using specific pads, the Livescribe pen allows you to write, and at the same time it is recording everything. Tapping the pen on the pad instantly starts audio recording. Later, by tapping the notes at a given point, it is possible to hear the audio recording of that section of the recording. All written work and audio recordings can be transferred to computer. Any drawings, graphics, etc. are replicated exactly as they are on the pads. Available at:

www.livescribe.com

Chapter 7

Assessment – Summary

Different routes

It is important for parents and teachers to appreciate that an assessment for dyslexia can take different routes, depending on the context and the objectives of the assessment. One type of assessment is not necessarily any better than another, but there are different forms of assessment and we have tried to highlight that in this book. Each may have different aims or approaches, and the rationale for the assessment can differ.

The main types of assessment are: school-based assessment, independent assessment, screening tests, and assessment for a singular purpose, such as examination accommodations. Additionally, some schools and authorities operate a staged process of identification/intervention, and the starting point of this can be classroom observation. This process may also be assisted by the education authority's educational psychologist.

It has already been noted in earlier chapters that classroom assessment can be more geared towards intervention and curriculum access. This is extremely important, and needs to be considered whatever the aims or purpose of the assessment. The outcome of classroom assessment can pave the way for differentiation, and for ensuring that the child is not left behind. This type of assessment can provide information on what to teach, and also how to teach the child. It can provide information on his or her learning preferences, and look at what has been tried before, how successful or otherwise the previous interventions were, and what should be done now. This type of assessment can be carried out by school personnel, and may be done jointly with the class teacher and the specialist support teacher. The parents can and should also be involved in this process.

Quite often, however, parents are looking for a formal diagnosis as well as the intervention that will probably be provided by the school as one of the outcomes from a school-based assessment. This should be made clear at the outset, although we do find that some schools are reluctant to formally diagnose dyslexia. They may prefer to wait until further down the line when it is clear that the child is not progressing as expected. In this case, of course, it may be too late, and the emotions of failure and the reality of low self-esteem may have taken hold.

Policy and practice

An important point to note is that highlighted in the website information arising from the Scottish government cross-party group on dyslexia. This indicates that 'receiving appropriate additional support when required is not dependent upon the formal identification of a specific label such as dyslexia'.

The Scottish government have in fact developed an 'Addressing Dyslexia Toolkit' (2017), which is a free online resource funded by the Scottish government, managed by Dyslexia Scotland and developed by the Toolkit Working Group. It is designed to support the 'Curriculum for Excellence' and 'Getting It Right for Every Child' (GIRFEC), and it provides information for teachers and local education authorities. It also provides guidance on the process of supporting, assessing and monitoring literacy difficulties, which can include dyslexia, and gives details of relevant approaches and strategies:

www.dyslexiascotland.org.uk/addressing-dyslexia-toolkit

However, this should not be interpreted to indicate that schools and local authorities are not supportive of formally identifying additional support needs such as dyslexia. This website provides a Scottish definition of dyslexia with a detailed explanation:

http://addressingdyslexia.org/what-dyslexia

Many authorites and countries operate a stage process system with early identification and intervention embedded. A good example of this is the USA where they have RTI (Response to Intervention) procedures. See:

www.understood.org/en/school-learning/special-services/rti/understanding-response-to-intervention

Early identification

Education authorities in the UK are keen to recognise the value of early identification. This is in fact recognised internationally – in the

USA, the RTI model is comprehensive, with early identification and early intervention at its core. Although there are variations of the RTI process, certain key components are present in all variations:

- universal screening

- progress monitoring

- high-quality, research-based instruction for all students in the general education classroom (Tier 1)

- further tiers of intervention targeting students who do not demonstrate adequate progress on screening or progress monitoring measures (Mellard and Johnson 2008).

Reid *et al.* (2005) reported on some very promising examples from Scotland, stemming from the results of government-supported research on dyslexia and SpLD – 'A Scotland-wide Audit of Education Authority Early Years Policies and Provision for Specific Learning Difficulties (SpLD) and Dyslexia'. A number of policy documents were obtained from different authorities in Scotland, and comments such as the following were commonplace in the research data: 'The authority indicated that they had a clear commitment to identifying children with dyslexia as early as possible.'

One of the first formal reports on early identification was the Republic of Ireland Report of the Task Force on Dyslexia (July 2001). This report also showed clear indicators of dyslexia for different age groups: 3–5 years, 5–7 years, 7–12 years and 12+. The report specifically indicated that there is a strong commitment to identifying dyslexia at an early age.

Weedon (2016) argues that through necessity early schooling places a great deal of emphasis on the acquisition of core literacy and numeracy skills – and for the children at risk of dyslexia this may be something that they cannot do quite as easily as would be expected. He observes that the 'happy' pre-school child becomes perhaps less happy in the early stages of education due to these factors and the expectations arising from them. If the child in the early years is experiencing significant difficulties acquiring literacy, the main issue would be to investigate why this is the case. This can involve looking at a number of factors, including:

- **sensory issues** such as hearing and vision; these factors need to be checked out as early as possible, as any distortion in either can restrict progress in reading

- the **level of teaching** and associated learner expectations

- the **school environment**, and whether the child feels relaxed and at ease, or perhaps tense

- the **classroom ethos** – is it too competitive or perhaps too relaxed and unstructured?

- the **teaching or reading programmes** being used may not be right for the child at that time

- reluctance to read or learn to read because of **learned helplessness** factors – that is, the child feeling overwhelmed by the task.

In England and Wales, *Special Educational Needs and Disability Code of Practice: 0 to 25 Years* (Department for Education and Department of Health and Social Care 2014) provides guidance on planning for learning and reviewing progress at the pre-school stage as well as the early years of school. This document emphasises the need to:

- **assess** – this involves carrying out an analysis of the child's needs, in collaboration with the parents; the initial assessment should be reviewed regularly, but if there is no progress then a fuller, specialist assessment should take place

- **plan** – evidence of effectiveness in the approaches to be used is the key here

- **do** – this would involve the early years teacher, in collaboration with the specialist, to oversee implementation of the programme that is to be put in place

- **review** – this is an important stage because it looks at the effectiveness of the support, and the progress that the child has made so far.

The independent assessment

This has also featured in this book, and the importance of this type of assessment in complementing any school-based assessment should not be overlooked. An independent assessment can provide a fresh perspective, and one that can focus in some detail on the diagnostic elements of an assessment. This type of assessment can include a range of tests, and these in combination can yield a learner profile. This profile in turn can point to a diagnosis, if appropriate. This type of assessment can also be used collaboratively with the school, and indeed the school may well have a school or education authority psychologist who can carry out the tests that would normally be used in an independent assessment.

If an independent psychologist is to be used by either the school or the parents, it is important to ensure that the person carrying out the assessment is professionally qualified. In the UK, that would mean being registered with the Health and Care Professions Council (HCPC). This organisation maintains standards and has a directory of registrants. See:

www.hcpc-uk.co.uk

In the USA each state would have a similar registration process and psychologists would need to meet the criteria set by the state. There is also guidance available from the American Psychological Association (APA), which is the largest scientific and professional organisation of psychologists in the USA, with around 117,500 members including scientists, educators, clinicians, consultants and students. They list all the State Licensing Boards, and psychologists should be registered with the Board in the area in which they practise. Details of each State Licensing Board are shown on this website:

https://www.apaservices.org/practice/ce/state/state-info.html?_ga=2.129564430.36570675.1547808494-2128867145.1547808494

Similarly in Canada, each of the provinces has a registration body and criteria. For example, in British Columbia it is the College of Psychologists of BC:

https://collegeofpsychologists.bc.ca

It is also important to ascertain that the psychologist has experience with dyslexia. Specialist teachers can also carry out assessments if they are specifically trained in this area and are recognised by a professional body. The SpLD Assessment Standards Committee (SASC) aims to promote and support best practice in the assessment of SpLDs. The authority for SASC, and its remit, stem from the SpLD Working Group 2005/Department for Education and Skills guidelines. SASC provides guidance on training, and implements standards for overseeing and approving processes of awarding SpLD Assessment Certificates. The following bodies provide accredited training:

- the British Dyslexia Association: www.bdadyslexia.org.uk

- PATOSS (Professional Association of Teachers of Students with Specific Learning Difficulties): www.patoss-dyslexia.org

- Communicate-ed: www.communicate-ed.org.uk

- Dyslexia Action: https://dyslexiaaction.org.uk

In the USA and Canada, assessment would normally be conducted by school psychologists or psychologists in private practice. Some training courses may be offered to teachers who have some training in psychometrics. For example, in New Zealand, LDANZ (Learning Difficulties Association of New Zealand) runs courses in assessment. See:

www.ldanz.org.nz/footerholder/training-options/assessor-training

If an independent assessment is used, then the psychologist will follow up with a formal written report. The nature, content and structure of this report will vary depending on the psychologist, but there are some general points that are usually followed, and these are detailed in Appendix 4.

Information from parents

It is important to involve parents in the assessment process as they can have a great deal of information to add. How the child is at home and at play is important and can provide a fuller picture which can help to develop a fuller assessment. An assessment is not only about achievements, but also about developing a profile of the learner that can inform intervention. The parents can also have an important role to play in intervention too – particularly in linking with the school.

It is also important to obtain information relating to the early years – this can include the period before school as well as the initial stages of schooling. Similarly, obtaining data on the child's sensory development – hearing and visual factors – is also important. For example, there is a connection between early intermittent hearing loss and dyslexia (Peer 2015).

Follow-up and follow-through

One of the important aspects about an assessment is the follow-up and particularly the recommendations on how to help the child or young person to develop and display his or her potential. This has been discussed in Chapter 6 on strategies and resources. Although this book is about assessment, we felt justified in including a chapter focusing on intervention, as we do see this as a key interlinking feature of assessment. The question 'what next?' should always be presented following an assessment.

We have endeavoured to include in this short book as much as possible to reflect the diversity of learners' needs, the range of assessment tools and procedures currently available, the nature of an assessment and the role of parents as well as that of the assessor, and importantly the range of strategies and resources that can be made available for learners with dyslexia. We hope that readers will find this book useful and that it can help to both demystify and simplify the assessment process. This can pave the way for early intervention and more successful outcomes for all with dyslexia.

References

American Psychiatric Association (APA) (2013) *Diagnostic and Statistical Manual of Mental Disorders (DSM-5)*. Fifth edition. Washington, DC: APA.

Bennett, L. and Ottley, P. (1997) *Launch into Reading Success through Phonological Awareness Training*. London: Harcourt.

Bishop, D.V.M. and Snowling, M.J. (2004) 'Developmental Dyslexia and Specific Language Impairment: Same or Different?' *Psychological Bulletin*, 7, 858–886.

Breznitz, Z. (2008) 'The Origin of Dyslexia: The Asynchrony Phenomenon.' In G. Reid, A. Fawcett, F. Manis and L. Siegel (eds) *The Sage Handbook of Dyslexia*. London: Sage.

Came, F. and Reid, G. (2008) *CAP It All: Concern, Assess, Provide. Practical Tools and Techniques to Identify and Assess Individual Needs*. Wiltshire: Learning Works International Ltd.

Campbell, A. (2009) *A Dyslexic Writes: An Essay on Dyslexia – A Conundrum of Conundrums*. Farnham: Helen Arkell Dyslexia Centre.

Department for Education and Department of Health and Social Care (2014) *Special Educational Needs and Disability Code of Practice: 0 to 25 Years*. Available at https://assets.publishing.service.gov.uk/government/uploads/system/uploads/attachment_data/file/398815/SEND_Code_of_Practice_January_2015.pdf (accessed 10/1/2019).

Dyslexia Scotland (2011) *Dyslexia and Us: A Collection of Personal Stories*. Stirling: Dyslexia Scotland.

Engelmann, S., Haddox, P. and Bruner, E. (1983) *Teach Your Child to Read in 100 Easy Lessons.* New York: Simon & Schuster.

Everatt, J. and Reid, G. (2009) 'An Overview of Recent Research.' In G. Reid (ed.) *The Routledge Dyslexia Companion*. London: Routledge.

Fawcett, A. (2017) *Procedural Learning Difficulties and Comorbidity in Dyslexia*. Paper presented at UNITE SpLD Conference, Singapore.

Fawcett, A. and Nicolson, R. (2008) 'Dyslexia and the Cerebellum.' In G. Reid, A. Fawcett, F. Manis and L. Siegel (eds) *The Sage Handbook of Dyslexia*. London: Sage.

Francks, C., MacPhie, I.L. and Monaco, A.P. (2002) 'The Genetic Basis of Dyslexia.' *The Lancet Neurology, Vol 1*.

Gathercole, S. (2018) *Supporting Learners: Where Does the Evidence Lead Us?* BDA International Conference, Telford, UK, March 2018.

Gilger, J.W. (2008) 'Some Special Issues Concerning the Genetics of Dyslexia: Revisiting Multivariate Profiles, Comorbidities, and Genetic Correlations.' In G. Reid, A. Fawcett, F. Manis and L. Siegel (eds) *The Sage Handbook of Dyslexia*. London: Sage.

Gray, A. (2016) 'English as an Additional Language (EAL): Special Educational Needs and Dyslexia. The Role of the 21st Century SENCo.' In L. Peer and G. Reid (eds) *Multilingualism, Literacy and Dyslexia: Breaking Down Barriers for Educators*. London: Routledge.

Guise, J., Reid, G., Lannen, S. and Lannen, C. (2016) 'Dyslexia and Specific Learning Difficulties: Assessment and Intervention in a Multilingual Setting.' In L. Peer and G. Reid (eds) *Multilingualism, Literacy and Dyslexia: Breaking Down Barriers for Educators.* London: Routledge.

Jeffries, S. and Everatt, J. (2004) 'Working Memory: Its Role in Dyslexia and Other Learning Difficulties.' *Dyslexia*, 10, 196–214.

Joshi, R.M. and Aaron, P.G. (2008) 'Assessment of Literacy Performance Based on the Componential Model of Reading.' In G. Reid, A. Fawcett, F. Manis and L. Siegel (eds) *The Sage Dyslexia Handbook.* London: Sage.

Kormos, J. and Smith, A.M. (2010) *Teaching Languages to Students with Specific Learning Differences*. Bristol: Multilingual Matters.

Kurnoff, S. (2000) *The Human Side of Dyslexia: 142 Interviews with Real People Telling Real Stories.* Monterey, CA: London Universal.

Landon, J. (2001) 'Inclusion and Dyslexia – The Exclusion of Bilingual Learners?' In L. Peer and G. Reid (eds) *Dyslexia: Successful Inclusion in the Secondary School.* London: David Fulton.

Mellard, D.F. and Johnson, E. (2008; online publication December 2013) *RTI: A Practitioner's Guide to Implementing Response to Intervention*. OnlineSage Publications. Available at http://sk.sagepub.com/books/rti (accessed 10/1/2019).

Molfese, D.L., Molfese, V.J., Barnes, M.E., Warren, C.G. and Molfese, P.J. (2008) 'Familial Predictors of Dyslexia: Evidence from Preschool Children with and without Familial Dyslexia Risk.' In G. Reid, A. Fawcett, F. Manis and L. Siegel (eds) *The Sage Dyslexia Handbook.* London: Sage.

Norton, E.S. and Wolf, M. (2012) 'Rapid Automatized Naming (RAN) and Reading Fluency: Implications for Understanding and Treatment of Reading Disabilities.' *Annual Review of Psychology*, 63, 11, 427–452.

Peer, L. (2015) 'Dyslexia, Bi/Multilingualism and Otitis Media (Glue Ear): A Sticky Educational Problem.' In L. Peer and G. Reid (eds) *Multilingualism, Literacy and Dyslexia: Breaking Down Barriers for Educators.* London: Routledge.

Reid, G., Deponio, P. and Davidson-Petch, L.D. (2005) 'Identification, Assessment and Intervention: Implications of an Audit on Dyslexia Policy and Practice in Scotland.' *Dyslexia*, 11, 3, 203–216.

Reid, G. and Guise, J. (2017) *Assessment for Dyslexia: From Early Years to Higher Education*. London: Bloomsbury.

Reid, G., Guise, N. and Guise, J. (2018) *The Big Book of Dyslexia Activities for Kids and Teens: 100 Creative, Fun, Multi-sensory and Inclusive Ideas for Successful Learning*. London: Jessica Kingsley Publishers.

Reid, G. and Kirk, J. (2001) *Dyslexia in Adults: Education and Employment*. Chichester: Wiley.

Republic of Ireland Task Force on Dyslexia (2001) *Report of the Task Force on Dyslexia*. Dublin: Government Publications. Available at www.sess.ie/sites/default/files/Dyslexia_Task_Force_Report_0.pdf (accessed 10/1/2019).

Rooke, M. (2016) *Creative, Successful, Dyslexic: 23 High Achievers Share their Stories*. London: Jessica Kingsley Publishers.

Rooke, M. (2018) *Dyslexia Is My Superpower (Most of the Time)*. London: Jessica Kingsley Publishers.

Rose, J. (2009) *Identifying and Teaching Children and Young People with Dyslexia and Literacy Difficulties*. London: Department for Children, Schools and Families.

SNAP, Special Educational Needs Assessment Profile (2018) Available at https://www.hoddereducation.co.uk/snap (accessed 22/2/2019). London: Hodder Education.

Snowling, M. (2017) *Dyslexia and Language Impairment*. Presentation at the Association for Child and Adolescent Mental Health, Cardiff, September 2017.

Stein, J. and The Dyslexia Research Trust (2014) 'The Genetics of Dyslexia.' *Dyslexia Daily*. Available at https://www.dyslexiadaily.com/blog/genetics-dyslexia (accessed 22/2/2019).

Stein, J. (2017) *The Dyslexia Debate*. Paper presented at the Learning Differences Convention, Melbourne and Sydney, March 2017.

Vellutino, F.R., Fletcher, J.M., Snowling, M.J. and Scanlon, D.M. (2004) 'Specific Reading Disability (Dyslexia): What Have We Learnt in the Past Four Decades?' *Journal of Child Psychology and Psychiatry*, 45, 1, 2–40.

Weedon, C. (2016) 'The Potential Impact and Influence of the Social Model of Disability.' In L. Peer and G. Reid (eds) *Special Educational Needs: A Guide for Inclusive Practice*. Second edition. London: Sage.

Wolf, B. and Berninger, V. (2015) 'Specific learning disabilities: Plural, definable, diagnosable, and treatable.' *Dyslexia Connections, International Dyslexia Association Newsletter for Parents*, 20 March.

Appendix 1

Tests Used in the Assessment of Dyslexia

Selection of tests used and overall rationale

The overall rationale for the assessment is based on current models of identifying learning difficulties as well as empirical research and guidance from *DSM-5*. It includes identifying discrepancies in the cognitive profile, particularly in the processing area – working memory and processing speed. It also includes an analysis of reading and spelling patterns, as well as expressive writing and writing speed, noting significant diagnostic discrepancies between scores.

Psychologist assessors have access to the WISC (Wechsler Intelligence Scale for Children) and WAIS (Wechsler Adult Intelligence Scale) tests, which cover a range of cognitive processes (verbal reasoning, non-verbal or visual-spatial abilities, working memory and processing speed). These are discussed below. Because all of the tests are contained in the same battery, it is possible to obtain a statistical measure of the differences between scores. That is, they can show statistically whether the difference between a (verbal or non-verbal) reasoning score and a processing score (speed or memory) is significant. One dyslexic profile often seen in dyslexia is described below.

The WISC and WAIS tests are correlated with the WIAT 3 tests that can be used to assess literacy and numeracy skills (these are discussed below). This means that the WISC 5 and WAIS 4 tests can also be used to find out whether the learner's literacy or maths attainments are at the level that would be expected, based on his or her cognitive reasoning scores. This can be particularly useful in identifying difficulties in pupils who are working at what appears to be an acceptable (usually average) level. It is possible using the WISC and WAIS tests to see whether that individual should perhaps be working at a higher-than-average level. It is also possible to see where a pupil is working at the expected level, but is having to put in extra effort and time to do this.

The Wide Range Intelligence Tests (WRIT) are available to teachers. They include tests of 'verbal intelligence' and 'visual intelligence'. They do not include tests for working memory or processing speed, and they are not correlated with tests in literacy attainment.

Cognitive tests

WECHSLER INTELLIGENCE SCALE FOR CHILDREN, FIFTH EDITION (WISC 5) (2016)

The WISC 5 is an individual test that does not require reading or writing.

Purpose of the test: The WISC 5 was designed as a measure of a child's intellectual ability.

Test age range: Ages 6.00 to 16.11 (six years old to 16 years and 11 months old).

Scores: Provides a full-scale IQ, and the following factor scores:

- verbal comprehension
- visual spatial
- fluid reasoning
- working memory
- processing speed.

Information: The WISC 5 is the fifth generation of the Wechsler Intelligence Scale for Children. Its predecessors, the WISC R, WISC 3 and WISC 4, were the most popular and widely researched test of children's intelligence in history.

Scoring: The average IQ is 100; 110–120 is viewed as high average, and over 120 is high. The average range is 90–110; below 90 the IQ is seen on the low average range, and below 79 the below average range. An IQ of around/below 70 is viewed as an indicator of severe learning difficulties. The distribution of scores can be seen in the figure on the next page.

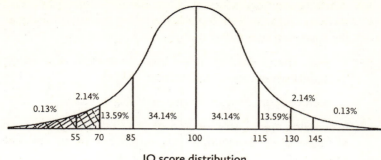

IQ score distribution

WISC 5 sub-tests are grouped by the following components:

- **Verbal comprehension** assesses the development of a child's language skills. It includes tests of expressive vocabulary, comprehension, reasoning and general knowledge. It includes the following core sub-tests:

  - **similarities**: concrete and abstract reasoning skills, categories and relationships, LTM (long-term memory)

  - **vocabulary**: the ability to express ideas verbally, word knowledge, LTM.

- **Visual spatial** assesses the development of a child's spatial analysis and the ability to analyse and synthesise information. It includes the following core sub-tests:

  - **block design**: spatial visualisation, analysis of a whole into its component parts

  - **visual puzzles**: ability to analyse and synthesise information.

- **Fluid reasoning** measures visual reasoning and quantitative reasoning and induction. It includes the following core sub-tests:

  - **matrix reasoning**: visual information-processing and abstract and reasoning skills

  - **figure weights**: measures quantitative reasoning and induction.

- **Working memory** assesses the student's auditory working memory and attention, and visual working memory. It includes the following core sub-tests:

  - **digit span**: recall of information (numbers), short-term auditory memory, concentration

  - **picture span**: measures visual working memory.

- **Processing speed** assesses motor (manual) skills and speed of information processing. It includes the following core sub-tests:

  - **coding**: paper and pencil task requiring the duplication of abstract designs – involves visual motor integration, speed of information-processing, short-term visual memory, visual tracking; this task can also be administered using an iPad rather than paper and pencil

  - **symbol search**: paper and pencil task – involves visual motor integration, speed of information-processing, visual tracking, short-term visual memory; this task can also be administered using an iPad rather than paper and pencil.

WECHSLER ADULT INTELLIGENCE SCALE, FOURTH EDITION (WAIS 4) (2008)

The WAIS 4 is the adult equivalent of the WISC 5 described above, and can be used with people aged 16 to 90 years. It provides a full-scale IQ, and the following factor scores:

- verbal comprehension

- perceptual reasoning

- working memory

- processing speed.

The sub-tests are grouped by scale membership as below:

- **Verbal comprehension** assesses the development of language skills. It includes tests of expressive vocabulary, comprehension, reasoning and general knowledge. It includes the following core sub-tests:

- **similarities**: concrete and abstract reasoning skills, categories and relationships, LTM (long-term memory)

- **vocabulary**: the ability to express ideas verbally, word knowledge, LTM

- **information**: general knowledge, LTM.

- **Perceptual reasoning** assesses the development of spatial analysis, and the ability to analyse and synthesise information, and measures visual reasoning, quantitative reasoning and induction. It includes the following core sub-tests:

  - **block design**: spatial visualisation, analysis of a whole into its component parts

  - **matrix reasoning**: visual information-processing and abstract and reasoning skills

  - **visual puzzles**: ability to analyse and synthesise information.

- **Working memory** assesses auditory working memory and attention. It includes the following core sub-tests:

  - **digit span**: recall of information (numbers), short-term auditory memory, concentration

  - **arithmetic**: attention, concentration, short-term auditory memory, numerical reasoning.

- **Processing speed** assesses motor (manual) skills and speed of information-processing. It includes the following core sub-tests:

  - **symbol search**: paper and pencil task – involves visual motor integration, speed of information processing, visual tracking, short-term visual memory; this task can also be administered using an iPad rather than paper and pencil

  - **coding**: paper and pencil task requiring the duplication of abstract designs – involves visual motor integration, speed of information-processing, short-term visual memory, visual tracking; this task can also be administered using an iPad rather than paper and pencil.

Cognitive profiles

There is a very wide range of possible cognitive profiles. The one described below is fairly typical in dyslexia, and it helps to illustrate the process of analysing where the strengths and weaknesses are, and how weaker areas might affect literacy attainments. It is very important to note that not every dyslexic learner will show this pattern of scores.

Verbal comprehension score is significantly higher than working memory score:

- processing is not keeping up with verbal abilities
- can lead to problems with learning attainments, getting thoughts down on paper, maintaining focus.

Verbal comprehension score is significantly higher than processing speed score:

- processing is not keeping up with verbal abilities
- can lead to problems with learning attainments, getting thoughts down on paper, maintaining focus.

Attainment tests

WECHSLER INDIVIDUAL ACHIEVEMENT TEST, THIRD EDITION (WIAT 3) (2017)

The WIAT 3 is one of the most comprehensive attainment tests, and as noted above it is correlated with the WISC 5 and the WAIS 4. This battery of tests is only available to appropriately qualified psychologists (a more restricted version – the WIAT 3-T – is available for teachers, and is noted in Table 2 below).

The WIAT 3 allows the psychologist assessor to compare attainment scores predicted on the basis of WISC 5 and WAIS 4 scores, with attainment scores actually achieved. So, it is possible to see if the student's performance in literacy or numeracy is at the expected level. It includes the following sub-tests:

- listening comprehension
- oral expression

- early reading skills
- word reading
- pseudo-word decoding
- oral reading fluency
- reading comprehension
- alphabet writing fluency
- sentence composition
- essay composition
- spelling
- numerical operations
- maths problem-solving
- maths fluency.

The WIAT 3 is of value because it separates the listening compre-hension measure into two sub-tests on receptive and expressive vocabulary. This can be useful in identifying those students who may have receptive or auditory processing issues, and also those with word-finding difficulties.

The WIAT 3 also has separate tests of maths reasoning and numeracy. The child with dyslexia may have a good understanding of maths concepts, but when it comes to processing the numbers and symbols, etc., they may have difficulties. These are likely to be apparent in the numeracy sub-test. The maths problem-solving test is administered one-to-one and it allows the assessor to see how it is that the student tackles more wordy problems, and ones where he or she has to figure out what calculation to do, as well as carrying out the calculation.

The WIAT 3 also has three sub-tests on maths fluency. These can provide particularly useful information for students with processing speed difficulties.

Some other tests might be added, or used in place of some of the WIAT 3 sub-tests, depending on the age and stage of the pupil, and what kind of evidence might be needed to obtain support or exam accommodations. These include the following:

GRAY ORAL READING TESTS (GORT-5)

The GORT-5 provides an efficient and objective measure of reading, and can aid the diagnosis of dyslexia. Four scores are provided:

- oral reading rate – the amount of time taken by a student to read texts aloud

- oral reading accuracy – the student's ability to pronounce each word correctly

- oral reading fluency – the student's rate and accuracy scores combined

- reading comprehension – the appropriateness of the student's responses to questions about the content of each story read.

The GORT-5 can provide useful diagnostic information, and any discrepancies between different aspects of reading can be noted. For example, there may be a difference between reading fluency and reading accuracy. If fluency is significantly below the level of reading accuracy, then this can provide some justification for extra time for reading. Similar comparisons can be made with the other scores from the GORT-5.

GRAY SILENT READING TEST (GSRT)

The GSRT provides a score for silent reading comprehension.

WIDE RANGE ACHIEVEMENT TEST (WRAT5)

The WRAT5 is a smaller battery of test that provides scores for:

- word reading
- spelling
- sentence comprehension
- mathematical computation.

COMPREHENSIVE TEST OF PHONOLOGICAL AWARENESS (CTOPP-2)

The CTOPP-2 tests can provide a phonological profile, and particularly useful data on phonological awareness. This is useful, because the research does indicate that this type of difficulty is a key factor in identifying dyslexia. The following sub-tests are available:

- elision
- blending words
- phoneme isolation
- memory for digits
- non-word repetition
- rapid digit naming
- rapid letter naming.

The CTOPP-2 rapid naming tests are oral, while in the WISC 5 and the WAIS 4, the processing speed tests involve writing or selecting items on an iPad. Useful comparisons can therefore be made between the performances in these two conditions.

RAPID AUTOMATISED NAMING (RAN) AND RAPID ALTERNATING STIMULUS (RAS) TESTS

The RAN/RAS tests might be used instead of the CTOPP-2 tests. They measure the child's speed of naming:

- objects
- colours
- numbers
- letters
- letters and numbers.

TEST OF WORD READING EFFICIENCY (TOWRE-2)

The TOWRE-2 tests measure the child's speed of reading sight words and non-words (phonemes) using the following sub-tests:

- sight word efficiency
- phonemic decoding efficiency.

WIDE RANGE ASSESSMENT OF MEMORY AND LEARNING (WRAML-2)

The WRAML-2 battery can be used to measure different aspects of the child's memory, using the following sub-tests:

- story memory
- design memory
- verbal learning
- picture memory
- number/letter memory.

It is important for parents and schools to be aware of the fact that tests are accessible to different categories of assessor, depending on that person's level of qualification. This can be seen in the Pearson criteria for accessing tests. Pearson Assessment publishes a wide variety of tests, and catalogue these by classifying them as CL3, CL2R, CL2 or CL1 instruments, depending on qualifications and training needed to use them:

- **CL3 tests** in general are those which do not require an individual to have advanced training in assessment and interpretation. Qualified teachers would be given this code.

- **CL2R tests** require qualified teaching status, and a further postgraduate qualification (Diploma or Masters) in SEN (Special Educational Needs). This qualification would need to be in SEN, SpLD or a relevant field.

- **CL2 tests** may be purchased by individuals who are certified by a professional organisation recognised by Pearson Assessment, or who have a graduate and/or postgraduate qualification relevant to their profession. This qualification code would encompass all psychologists other than those mentioned for CL1, speech or occupational therapists, mental health professionals, and health practitioners with appropriate graduate and professional qualifications in their field of practice.

- **CL1 tests** can be used by anyone who is registered with the Health and Care Professions Council (HCPC) as a practitioner psychologist and/or is a chartered psychologist with the British Psychological Society (BPS).

Tables 1 and 2 highlight the tests/areas that can be looked at in a school assessment, and what the results may imply. The table represents only a selection of tests that can be used by teachers at school – it is important also to refer to the bullet points above on the prerequisite qualifications necessary to access these tests.[1]

---

1   Please see https://www.pearsonclinical.com/psychology/qualifications.html for the qualifications in North America.

Table 1: Selected CL3 tests that can be used at school

(Note: CL3 tests can be used by most teachers)

Test	Qualification level	Reasons for use	Implications
York Assessment of Reading Comprehension (YARC) Ages 4 to 16	N/A	Measures reading skills in early years, and passage reading at school level	Uses UK norms; can be used as a benchmark as it also assesses accuracy and reading rate
Gray Silent Reading Tests (GSRT) Ages 7 to 25	CL3	Measure silent reading comprehension and are untimed	Can be a useful comparison with performances in timed tests; focuses on understanding; silent reading; can be a good measure for children with dyslexia
Gray Oral Reading Tests (GORT-5) Ages 6 to 23 years 11 months	CL3	Provide information on reading speed, accuracy and reading comprehension; incorporate a miscue analysis procedure which helps to identify the type of reading errors made	A good measure of all three aspects of reading; as it means reading aloud and is timed, it gives a good measure of confidence in reading
Test of Word Reading Efficiency (TOWRE-2) Ages 6 to 24 years 11 months	CL3	Measures accuracy and fluency in word reading	This is a timed test; it can also provide information on speed of accessing print, and decoding skills
Dyslexia Early Screening Test (DEST) Ages 4 years 6 months to 6 years 5 months	CL3	Looks at early reading skills, working memory and speed and other strong indicators of dyslexia	Can be very useful in flagging up children who may need further assessment; can be incorporated into a school's early identification policy
Dyslexia Screening Test – Junior (DST-J) Ages 6 years 6 months to 11 years 5 months	CL3	Identifies children in this age range who are at risk of dyslexia	Very useful in early identification and as a general school screening tool
Dyslexia Screening Test – Secondary (DST-S) Ages 11 years 6 months to 16 years 5 months	CL3	Includes reading, verbal and semantic fluency, decoding and non-verbal reasoning	Useful for those children who have not been identified previously, but are experiencing dyslexic-type difficulties

LUCID Rapid Ages 4 to 15	N/A	Whole-class screening for dyslexia; looks at phonological processing (4–15 years), working memory (4–15 years), phonic decoding skills (8–15 years), visual-verbal integration memory (4–7 years)	Can be used for early identification, as well as obtaining diagnostic information; can point to the need for further testing
Comprehensive Test of Phonological Processing (CTOPP-2) Ages 4 to 24 years 11 months	CL3	Tests key aspects in decoding and phonological processing, as well as phonological memory and processing speed	Can identify phonological problems, and these can be key indicators in dyslexia
Detailed Assessment of Speed of Handwriting (DASH) Ages 9 to 16 years 11 months	CL3	Assesses handwriting speed – contains five sub-tests on different aspects of handwriting speed	Useful for providing evidence for access arrangements for early-stage curriculum tests and general qualifications
Launch into Reading Success (Bennett and Ottley 1997) Ages 2 to 12	CL3	Auditory training programme beginning with single words as units of sound and concluding with linkage	Photocopiable exercises can pinpoint the areas where the child may need help

Table 2: Popular specialised tests (CL2R)

Test	Qualification level	Reasons for use	Implications
The WIAT 3 UK edition for teachers (WIAT 3 UK-T) Ages 4 to 25	CL2R	UK-normed battery of five sub-tests to examine key aspects of literacy: word reading, reading comprehension and spelling	Can provide useful information on reading levels, and diagnostic information through analyses of the type of errors made in reading and spelling
Wide Range Achievement Test (WRAT5) Ages 5 to 85+	CL2R	Measures the basic academic skills of reading, spelling, sentence comprehension and maths computation	Can provide an alternative to the WIAT 3 – takes less time to administer, and provides a useful, structured sub-test on sentence comprehension

Appendix 2

Glossary of Terms

ADHD – children with ADHD (Attention Deficit Hyperactivity Disorder) will have a short attention span and tend to work on a number of different tasks at the same time. They will be easily distracted, and may have difficulty settling in some classrooms, particularly if there are a number of competing distractions. It is also possible for some children to have attention difficulties without hyperactivity. This is referred to as ADD (Attention Deficit Disorder).

Auditory discrimination – many children with dyslexia can have difficulties with auditory discrimination. This refers to difficulties in identifying specific sounds, and in distinguishing these sounds from other similar sounds. This can be associated with the phonological difficulties experienced by children with dyslexia (see 'phonological awareness' below). Hearing loss, or partial and intermittent hearing loss, can also be associated with difficulties in auditory discrimination.

Automaticity – this refers to the situation when the learner obtains a degree of mastery over the skill or information that is being learnt. In the case of reading, this would be automatic word recognition without the need to actively decode the word, although it would also be important for the learner to achieve automaticity in decoding so that he or she would know automatically how to decode a new word. It can apply to any skill that has to be learnt.

Cognitive – this refers to the learning and thinking process. It describes how learners take in information, and how they retain and understand the information.

Decoding – this refers to the reading process and specifically to the breaking down of words into the individual sounds.

Differentiation – this is the process of adapting materials and teaching to suit a range of learners' abilities and level of attainments. Usually, differentiation refers to the task, the teaching, the resources and the assessment. Each of these areas can be differentiated to suit the needs of individuals or groups of learners.

Dyscalculia – this describes difficulties in numeracy. This could be due to difficulties in the computation of numbers, retaining numbers while carrying out calculations, or reading the instructions associated with number problems.

Dysgraphia – this relates to difficulties in handwriting. Some children with dyspraxia (see below) and dyslexia may also show signs of dysgraphia. Children with dysgraphia will often benefit from using lined paper as they often have visual/spatial problems, and they may have an awkward pencil grip.

Dyslexia – this refers to difficulties in accessing print, but there are also other factors such as memory, processing speed, sequencing, directions, syntax, spelling and written work that can be challenging. Children with dyslexia often have phonological difficulties which result in poor word attack skills. In many cases, they require a dedicated intervention programme.

Dyspraxia – this refers to co-ordination difficulties. It can also be described as Developmental Co-ordination Disorder (DCD). More information can be found on the Dyspraxia Foundation website (see, for example, https://dyspraxiafoundation.org.uk/about-dyspraxia/dyspraxia-glance).

Eye-tracking – this is the skill of being able to read a line and keep the eyes on track throughout the line. Children with poor eye-tracking may omit lines or words on a page. Sometimes, masking a part of a line or page, or using a ruler, can help with eye-tracking.

Fluid reasoning – this is the child's ability to work out the underlying relationships between visual objects, and to use reasoning to identify rules, and apply them.

Hyperlexia – this is the opposite of dyslexia in that the hyperlexic learner would typically be extremely skilled in decoding and reading words. However, there can be difficulties with comprehension of text.

Information-processing – this describes how children and adults learn new information. It is usually described as a cycle – input, cognition and output. Children with dyslexia can have difficulties at all the stages of information-processing and dyslexia can be referred to as a difficulty or a difference in information-processing.

Learning disabilities – this is a general term, mainly used in North America, to describe the range of specific learning difficulties such as dyslexia, dyspraxia, dyscalculia and dysgraphia. Often referred to as LD, it is not equated with intelligence, and children with LD are usually in the average to above-average intelligence range.

Learning styles – this term can describe the student's preferences for learning. This can be using visual, auditory, kinaesthetic or tactile stimuli, but it can also relate to environmental preferences such as sound, the use of music when learning, preferences for time of day and working in pairs, groups or individually. There is a lot of literature on learning styles, but the concept is still seen as quite controversial – very probably because there are hundreds of different instruments, all of which claim to measure learning styles, and many learners are in fact quite adaptable, and can adjust to different types of learning situations and environments. Nevertheless, it is a useful concept to apply in the classroom, particularly for children with learning difficulties, because if we consider learning styles it is more possible to identify their strengths, and to use these in preparing materials and in teaching.

Long-term memory – this is used to recall information that has been learnt and needs to be recalled for a purpose. Many children with dyslexia can have difficulty with long-term memory as they have not organised the information they have learnt. Recalling it can be challenging as they may not have enough cues to assist with this process. Also, working memory can play a role in storage and retrieval, and this means there can be some delay in getting things into and out of long-term memory. Study skills programmes can help with long-term memory.

Metacognition – this is the process of thinking about thinking; that is, being aware of how one learns and how a problem was solved. It is a process-focused approach and one that is necessary for effective and efficient learning. Many children with dyslexia may have poor metacognitive awareness because they are unsure of the process of learning. For that reason, study skills programmes can be useful.

Multi-sensory – this refers to the use of a range of modalities in learning. In this context, 'multi-sensory' usually refers to the use of visual, auditory, kinaesthetic and tactile learning. It is generally accepted that children with dyslexia need a multi-sensory approach that utilises all of these modalities.

Neurological – this refers to brain-associated factors. This could be brain structure – that is, the different components of the brain – or brain processing – that is, how the components interact with each other. The research in dyslexia shows that both brain structure and brain-processing factors are implicated in dyslexia.

Peer tutoring – this happens when two or more children work together and try to learn from each other. It may also be the case that an older, more proficient learner is working (as tutor) with a younger, less accomplished learner (as tutee).

Phonological awareness – this term refers to the process of becoming familiar with the letter sounds and letter combinations that make the sounds in reading print. There are 44 sounds in the English language, and some sounds are very similar. This can be confusing and challenging for children with dyslexia. They often get the sounds confused, or have difficulty in retaining and recognising them when reading, or in speech.

Specific Learning Difficulties (SpLDs) – this term refers to the range of difficulties experienced by some learners. These difficulties can involve skills of reading, co-ordination, spelling, written expression and handwriting. There are quite a number of SpLDs, and they can be seen as being distinct from general learning difficulties. Children with general learning difficulties usually find most areas of the curriculum challenging, and may have a lower level of comprehension than children with SpLDs, who by definition will have comparative areas of strength.

Visual spatial abilities – these relate to the ability to successfully plan and design visual tasks. Children with skills here will have a good awareness of space and how objects can fit together.

Working memory – this is the first stage in short-term memory. It involves the learner holding information in short-term store and carrying out a processing activity simultaneously. This can be solving a problem, reading instructions or taking notes from the board or from speech. Children with dyslexia often experience difficulties with working memory.

Appendix 3

Useful Contacts

UK

Bangor Miles Dyslexia Centre: www.dyslexia.bangor.ac.uk
British Dyslexia Association: www.bdadyslexia.org.uk
Dr Gavin Reid: www.drgavinreid.com
Dysguise Ltd: www.dysguise.com
Dyslexia Centre North West: www.dyslexiacentrenorthwest.co.uk
Dyslexia Scotland: www.dyslexiascotland.org.uk
Dyspraxia Foundation: https://dyspraxiafoundation.org.uk
Helen Arkell Centre: www.arkellcentre.org.uk
Iansyst Ltd: www.iansyst.co.uk and www.dyslexic.com
National Attention Deficit Disorder Information Service: www.addiss.co.uk
Northern Ireland Dyslexia Association: www.nida.org.uk
Nottingham Dyslexia Association: www.dyslexia.uk.net
Professional Association of Teachers of Students with SpLDs: www.patoss-
    dyslexia.org

USA and Canada

Canada Dyslexia Association: www.dyslexiaassociation.ca
Dyslexic Advantage: www.dyslexicadvantage.org
International Dyslexia Association: www.interdys.org
Learning Difficulties Association of Canada: www.ldac-acta.ca
Learning Disabilities Association of America: www.ldaamerica.org
REACH Learning Centre, Vancouver, Canada: www.reachlearningcentre.com

Rest of the world

Australian Dyslexia Association: http://dyslexiaassociation.org.au

Dyslexia Association (Hong Kong): www.dyslexia.org.hk

Dyslexia Association of Ireland: www.dyslexia.ie

Dyslexia Association of Singapore: www.das.org.sg

Dyslexia Foundation of New Zealand: www.dyslexiafoundation.org.nz

European Dyslexia Association: www.eda-info.eu

Learning Differences Convention, Australia: www.learningdifference convention.com

Lighthouse Learning Centre, Cairo, Egypt: www.llcegypt.com

Appendix 4

Interpreting an Assessment Report

The potential of a full and formal psychologist or specialist teacher report is considerable. It can document the learning profile of the child, and formally describe strengths and weaknesses. Moreover, the report can provide a diagnosis, and this may well make a difference to the outcome and subsequent intervention for the child. It can also give hope and encouragement to parents, and this is extremely important. Some parents, however, do find the report confusing due to the technical language, and the detail of the descriptions of some of the tests and sub-tests used. We have already described some of the more popular tests in this book, but here we want to comment on the individual components that can be found in most reports.

We do not provide a sample report simply because reports can differ, although in the UK, the SpLD Assessment Standards Committee (SASC) has developed a formal structure for reports for students in further and higher education that assessors are expected to comply with. SASC also provides a description of the tests that should be used. These guidelines are extremely helpful for those conducting assessments in further and higher education. They are regularly updated and revised and are available at:

www.sasc.org.uk/SASCDocuments/SpLD_Working_Group_2005-DfES_Guidelines.pdf

www.sasc.org.uk/SASCDocuments/REVISED%20guidelines-March%202016%20a.pdf

At present, however, there is a considerable variation in the reports on assessment of children pre-16. It is expected, however, that by April 2020 SASC will have issued guidelines to bring some uniformity and consistency into pre- and post-16 reports, utilising the results of a survey that was initiated in March 2019.

In the USA and Canada, reports usually conform to the criteria for diagnosis set out in *DSM-5* as well as the Provincial Ministry of Education in Canada and the State and School Boards in the USA:

www.nasbe.org/about-us/state-boards-of-education

Below are some of the key areas that should be included in a report, and what these mean. The wording and the order of these topic headings can differ.

Contents of the assessment report
Information and registration details of the psychologist or specialist teacher assessor
This is important because it allows you to check that the assessor is fully registered, and with whom. It is also important to include the assessor's contact details because you may have questions that arise some time after the assessment.

Important dates
The report should include the child's age and date of birth, the date of testing and the date of the report. It is important to check these to ensure all is correct.

Test conditions and test information
This would include information on the test environment, for example the length of the test and how the child responded. It would also include a list of the tests used. Details of the test used may be included in an appendix to the report.

Background information
This would include details of the child's challenges and strengths as they are known at that time. It is often useful if this part of the report briefly refers to early history, for example if the child was late in reading, had a change of schools, etc. It can also be useful to have some information about the current school and if any additional intervention is being received.

Reason for referral

It is important to state why the child is being assessed. This information would often be provided by the parents or the referring agency.

Summary

This should be near the beginning of the report, and should be a concise statement indicating the implications of the results, any diagnosis to emerge from the assessment and the nature of recommendations and/or accommodations that could be made.

Results

This would normally be divided into the results of ability tests, and attainment tests.

Ability tests in psychologist reports would tend to be taken from the WISC 5 or WAIS 4 IQ tests. It is important to appreciate that the actual IQ score is not necessarily the most important piece of information, and indeed it can be misleading in the child who is dyslexic. The reason is that his or her profile is likely to show differences across the scores – for example, having a lower working memory than verbal comprehension score. In this example, the working memory score pulls the average down, so that the overall score is not likely to fully reflect that child's ability. The full-scale IQ score is usually not included in the report for that reason. The profile to emerge from the IQ tests is more important in an assessment for learning difficulties.

The author of the report would be likely to draw attention to any discrepancies that might exist between reasoning scores and processing scores because this can be meaningful for a diagnosis, and for pinpointing intervention (an example of these discrepancies has been given in Chapter 4 in the section 'Discrepancies and variations in scores').

Specialist teacher assessors do not have access to the WISC 5 or WAIS 4 tests, and instead they will measure underlying ability, processing speed and working memory using different test batteries.

The results section would also include the results of attainment tests. This would include tests of reading, spelling and expressive writing, and often also tests of maths and handwriting. Reading can be assessed in terms of accuracy, fluency (speed) and comprehension. All of those areas are important. Maths can be assessed in terms of numeracy skills, speed of calculation and maths reasoning. There may also be additional tests of phonological processing speed and memory – depending on the child's age and the challenges experienced.

Discussion of results

This can be a confusing part for parents, because the language used in interpreting the results may be quite technical. Essentially, this section should look at the implications of the assessment results. For example, if the child has a low processing speed, this can have an impact on reading speed, reading comprehension and maths speed and accuracy. If there is a diagnosis offered, then this section should be able to justify that, and indicate which results can be associated with dyslexia. The reasons for the diagnosis of dyslexia should be given here.

Summary and conclusions

This is normally a short section and essentially should summarise the main points of the assessment and the main conclusion. Some specific pointers for intervention can also be given here.

Recommendations

This is often the part that interests parents most. It should contain suggestions for interventions and strategies for the areas the child was weak in. Recommendations do not need to be confined to the learner's weak areas, and some good practice in teaching and learning can be included in this section. It is also a good idea to suggest some apps and websites to give parents some choice in what to look for. It is very likely that the report will be sent to the school, so some of the recommendations may well be more geared for the school than the home.

Appendices

The appendices may contain the actual result tables, or these may be inserted into the body of the text. The description of the tests used might be included in an appendix. There may also be a glossary of the key terms used in the report. Some examples of terms that can be used in the appendix are shown below.

Some technical terms explained

Confidence interval – there is a margin of error in all formal testing. The 95 per cent confidence interval allows us to be 95 per cent confident that the individual's 'true' score would fall within that range of scores. Where confidence intervals for different tests do not overlap, this can indicate a difference between the scores that is worthy of note.

DSM-5 – this is the term used to refer to the manual used by clinicians and researchers to diagnose and classify mental disorders. The American Psychiatric Association (APA) published DSM-5 in 2013, at the end of a 14-year revision process. It has codes for different learning difficulties, and these are:

- 315.00 With impairment in reading
- 315.2 With impairment in written expression
- 315.1 With impairment in mathematics.

General ability index – the general ability index discounts the processing scores (processing speed and working memory). So it provides an indication of ability based only on the reasoning scores (verbal reasoning, and visual reasoning including visual spatial ability). For children with dyslexia this score can be more useful than the full-scale IQ score, because if a child has a lower score for processing (working memory and/or processing speed), this lowers the full-scale IQ score, so that it does not fully reflect their underlying ability.

Level of significance – the significance level of 0.05 (written as $p < 0.05$) means that there are only five chances in a hundred that the result could have happened by coincidence, and that the result is unusual. The significance level of 0.01 (written as $p < 0.01$) means that there is only one chance in a hundred that the result could have happened by coincidence, and that the result is very unusual.

Percentile – this is the individual's rank within a group of same-age peers. A percentile rank expresses the proportion of scores that fall below a particular score. A score at the 27th percentile, for example, means that the individual's score was higher than 27 per cent of other individuals the same age. Scores between the 25th and 74th percentile are in the average range. A score at the 50th percentile is in the middle of the average range.

Standard deviation – this is the average deviation (difference) from the mean, regardless of direction. When the mean (or average) is 100, one standard deviation is generally considered to be 15 points.

Standard score – this relates an individual to his or her contemporaries in a standard way, that always means the same thing at any age. Average standard scores fall between 90 and 110, and these represent the middle 50 per cent (half) of the population at the particular age. The mid-point standard score of the average range is 100.

Statistical significance – a statistically significant score occurs when there is an unusually large difference between two scores.

Visual spatial abilities – these relate to the ability to successfully plan and design visual tasks. Children with skills here will have a good awareness of space and how objects can fit together.

Working memory – this involves holding two or more pieces of information at any one time and simultaneously undertaking a processing activity. It should be noted that, in the WISC 5 tests, the overall working memory score is made up of sub-tests in auditory working memory (digit span) and visual memory (picture span), and it can be important to consider these separately. The child may have more skills and score higher in picture memory. This can improve the overall score, and he or she might have difficulties in auditory working memory that might be significant in his or her learning.

About the Authors

Dr Gavin Reid is an international practitioner psychologist, consultant and author. He was a classroom teacher and university lecturer, and has written over 30 books in the field of dyslexia and learning. His books have been translated into seven languages. He currently lectures worldwide, and has regular international consultancies. Dr Reid is Chair of the British Dyslexia Association Accreditation Board. He has sat on government panels on assessment and dyslexia, and has been engaged in a number of United Nations-funded projects as a learning difficulties expert on assessment and practice for dyslexia.

Dr Jennie Guise is a practitioner psychologist, author and founder of Dysguise Ltd. She has worked as a university lecturer, and also has extensive experience of working with children at school level. She works in the UK and internationally, carrying out independent assessments for parents, schools, colleges, universities and corporate clients, and providing seminars and workshops on dyslexia and related issues.

Index